DISCARD

```
LB
1029    Kapfer
.N6       Preparing and using
K36       individualized
          learning packages...
```

PREPARING AND USING INDIVIDUALIZED LEARNING PACKAGES

for Ungraded, Continuous Progress Education

Philip G. Kapfer, Ph.D.
University of Utah
Salt Lake City, Utah

Glen F. Ovard, Ed.D.
Brigham Young University
Provo, Utah

EMPHASIZING:

> *Concepts*
> *Behavioral Objectives*
> *Individualized Learning Materials and Activities*
> *Pre-, Self-, and Post-Assessment Methods*
> *Quest*

MODELS PROVIDED FOR:

> *Managing Continuous Progress Education*
> *Preparing Individualized Learning Packages*

Copyright © 1971 Educational Technology Publications, Englewood Cliffs, New Jersey 07632.

All rights reserved. This book or parts thereof may not be reproduced in any form or by any means, electronic or mechanical, including photocopying, recording, or by any information storage and retrieval system, without written permission of the authors and the publisher.

Printed in the United States of America.

Library of Congress Catalog Card Number: 73-125877.

International Standard Book Number: 0-87778-015-3.

First Printing.

PREFACE

Many educators have been intimately involved in attempting to bring about substantive changes in schools. The results of such efforts can be observed readily in new approaches to physical facilities, staffing patterns, and the organization and scheduling of students. However, recent *curricular* changes have brought about much more significant modifications in the behaviors and roles of administrators, teachers, and students in elementary and secondary schools.

A few schools, during the past ten or fifteen years, have provided much of the leadership for change. Such schools have inaugurated team teaching, non-grading, flexible scheduling, the "Trump Plan," and various other organizational strategies in an attempt to provide students with opportunities for greater self-initiative and self-direction in learning. The reason given most frequently for trying these various tools and strategies was to better individualize instruction and learning.

However, in the initial implementation of organizational changes in elementary and secondary schools, students were usually still being guided by the same kinds of curricular and instructional strategies which had been employed in self-contained classrooms by a single teacher in a group-oriented situation of twenty-five or thirty students. In such situations, organizational changes usually produced one of two results—they precipitated much needed *curricular* change or they simply reverted back to more traditional patterns of management. In those cases where curricular change eventually resulted, educators hoped to provide students with honest opportunities for individual involvement and responsibility.

During this process of change, traditional curricular practices were examined much more critically than heretofore. It became obvious that both instructional materials and learning strategies were inappropriately organized for individualizing the educational program in schools. We began to recognize the need for unique curricular vehicles designed to translate curriculum guides and traditional teacher lesson plans into the kind of student lesson plans which would serve as road maps to guide the student in his learning. For convenience in communication, we began to call this type of curricular vehicle an Individualized Learning Package (or an ILP).

Our next step was to discuss at great length the purposes of ILPs in terms of individualizing. We felt that ILPs should be designed to provide for several aspects of individualized instruction and learning. First, ILPs should provide for continuous progress learning. In other words, ILPs should permit students to learn at their own unique rates, rather than at rates imposed by teachers for the purpose of group-paced instruction.

Second, ILPs should offer the student alternative ways of achieving stated behavioral objectives; students should be able to select from commercially available and teacher-prepared learning media of all types. In this way, students can be allowed to take advantage of and expand on their own learning strategies.

Third, ILPs should permit students, with the help of teachers, to plan their own learning sequences. As a result, students should be given the opportunity, whenever feasible, of taking advantage of their own interests and motivations.

ILPs also should provide for individual differences in ability by directing students to materials which are aimed at a variety of difficulty levels. Such alternatives might include a range of reading levels and conceptual sophistication as well as a variety of subject matter content.

Finally, ILPs should provide for successful learning experiences at varying levels of self-initiative and self-direction. By means of such experiences, students should learn to increasingly value independent study and learning.

To summarize, the primary purpose of ILPs is to assist teachers in creating more humanized learning environments. In such environments, the teacher's role, rather than being one of presenting information, becomes one of facilitating or managing a total environment for learning. In his new role, the teacher spends much more time talking *with* students as individuals and in small groups rather than talking *at* them in groups of twenty, fifty, or one hundred. This book presents the ILP approach to instructional management through curriculum design.

We owe a great debt of thanks to the many elementary and secondary teachers with whom we worked while serving as consultants throughout the United States. We owe even more to those teachers and administrators with whom we worked on a longitudinal basis. The faith, time, and energy of these people helped us transform ideas into actions, thus making this book possible. Some of the educators who greatly influenced our thinking during frequent encounters and discussions were Dr. Allan A. Glatthorn, Eugene R. Howard, Dr. B. Claude Mathis, R. Herbert Ringis, Dr. James E. Smith, Gardner A. Swenson, Dr. J. Lloyd Trump, and Wm. H. Wallin. The contributions of faculty members at Valley High School and Ruby S. Thomas Elementary School in Las Vegas, Nevada, and the B.Y.U. Campus Laboratory School, Provo, Utah, are recognized with thanks.

Special appreciation and recognition are due Dr. Miriam B. Kapfer, who made substantive contributions to the book's content, designed the final layout, and creatively edited the manuscript in all its stages of development.

January, 1971   P.G.K.
                                                                                 G.F.O.

CONTENTS

PREFACE iii

CONTENTS v

A CRITICAL INTRODUCTION vii

PART I.   INDIVIDUALIZING INSTRUCTION AND LEARNING
          INVOLVEMENT IS THE KEY!

          ILP 1. A View of Individualized Instruction and
                  Continuous Progress Education 3

PART II. CURRICULAR COMPONENTS
          HERE ARE THE PIECES!

          ILP 2. What Will Be Learned? 33
                  Concept, Skill, and Value Statements
          ILP 3. What Changes Will Occur? 65
                  Learning Objectives
          ILP 4. What Will Facilitate Those Changes? 101
                  Individualized Learning Materials and Activities
          ILP 5. What Can Evaluation Do to Help? 139
                  Pre-, Self-, and Post-Assessment

ILP 6. What Comes Next? 167
        Quest

PART III. **ORGANIZING THE COMPONENTS**
          PUTTING THE PIECES TOGETHER!

ILP 7. Organizing for Alternative Instructional and
        Learning Approaches 189
ILP 8. New Teacher-Learner Roles in an Individualized
        Learning Package System 223

PART IV. **EVALUATION FOR DECISION AND ACTION**
         IMPROVEMENT NEVER ENDS!

ILP 9. Evaluating the Individualized Curriculum and
        the Continuous Progress System 239

A CRITICAL INTRODUCTION

You should read this page. Why do we say this? Because this book is different!

It is different because it takes a new approach to designing and using curriculum materials. It is different because the style and method of the book combine several of the most promising new approaches to curriculum development and writing. It is different because it develops a means whereby materials for an ungraded, individualized curriculum can be created and used within the present structure of our school systems. Because the book "practices what it preaches," it is written in a format which is different from that usually found in textbooks. In brief, it is written in Individualized Learning Packages (ILPs).

The ILP curricular design developed here accommodates ideas such as conceptual approaches to knowledge; learning based on specific objectives; independent study for all students; continuous progress education; exploration, guided discovery, and presentation approaches to content; and learning principles such as reinforcement, motivation, and transfer.

But, let us take one step at a time. The basic ingredients from which ILPs are built include the following:

(1) concept, skill, or value statements,

(2) specific learning objectives,

(3) alternative learning activities—including media and methods of all types, selected according to the content and strategy of instruction and learning,

(4) assessment, evaluation, or testing—including pre-, self-, and post-assessment methods, and

(5) quest in breadth and in depth.

As we already stated, this book is different. It is organized into Individualized Learning Packages rather than chapters. We have just seen the five basic ingredients from which the curricular design of an ILP is built. Now, let us take a brief look at how the basic ingredients are put together. Most ILPs in this book are constructed in the following sequence: (1) a concept statement for the entire ILP, (2) a list of the sub-concept statements for the entire ILP, (3) a list of the learning objectives for the entire ILP, (4) instructions concerning a pre-test which covers all the learning objectives for the ILP, (5) one or more lessons into which the sub-concepts and learning objectives may be divided, (6) instructions concerning a post-test which covers all the learning objectives for the ILP, and (7) suggestions for quest.

The lessons which are incorporated into each ILP also have their own typical sequence of curricular ingredients. The sub-concepts and learning objectives which are identified at the beginning of the ILP are repeated in the lessons to which they apply. Next come directions which usually relate to the alternative learning activities which follow. Finally, the lesson concludes with a self-test and key after the heading, "Check Your Progress."

An explanation of the organization within each ILP is needed prior to your entering ILP 1 (or any other ILP in this book, should you wish to follow a different sequence from ours). An ILP typically contains some information designed specifically for the teacher and some for the student. For your convenience, we have placed the student ILP materials on right-hand pages. All instructions to the student are set in bold face italics. All supplementary materials including commentary, additional references, and teacher-administered tests and test keys are included on left-hand pages.

Now turn to your first ILP. (You will notice that there is a good deal of space on most pages of this book; *use* this space to insert your own comments, questions, and answers—become *involved*!)

PART I: **INDIVIDUALIZING INSTRUCTION AND LEARNING**
INVOLVEMENT IS THE KEY !

ILP 1

A VIEW OF INDIVIDUALIZED INSTRUCTION AND CONTINUOUS PROGRESS EDUCATION

CONCEPT

A continuous progress curriculum provides for individual differences.

SUB-CONCEPTS

An individualized, continuous progress curriculum allows each student to progress at his own best rate of speed commensurate with his abilities, interests, needs, and motivational patterns.

Individualized instruction and learning can occur when the curriculum and the materials and activities are organized for self-pacing through Individualized Learning Packages (ILPs).

LEARNING OBJECTIVES

You should be able to write a definition of an individualized, continuous progress curriculum.

You should be able to state at least three ways in which an individualized, continuous progress curriculum can provide for differences among learners.

You should be able to list the basic ingredients found in an ILP.

PRE-TEST FOR ILP 1

(1) Write a definition of the concept of individualized continuous progress education.

(2) State at least three ways in which such a curriculum provides for individual differences.

(3) List five basic ingredients of an ILP.

Have you read the critical introduction beginning on page vii? If you have not, you may wish to do so now.

If you have also read the concept, sub-concepts, and learning objectives for this ILP, you are ready to take the pre-test (opposite page). Pre-tests are designed to determine (1) whether you know all the material already and should begin with a different ILP, (2) whether you know so little about the material in the ILP that you should begin with a different ILP, (3) whether you know some of the material and, with teacher consultation, can skip some parts of the ILP, or (4) whether you should complete all of the ILP.

After you have taken the pre-test, consult with your teacher for help in deciding whether you should go on with all or part of this ILP or whether you should choose another ILP. Of course, if you are using this book without assistance from a teacher, you will need to make your own decision based on the information provided in the pre-test key (next page).

PRE-TEST KEY FOR ILP 1

(1) An individualized, continuous progress curriculum is an ungraded curriculum which allows the learner to proceed through what is to be learned at his own rate of speed commensurate with his abilities, interests, needs, and motivational patterns.

(2) An individualized, continuous progress curriculum provides for student differences through (a) individual selection of learning materials, (b) learner-regulated rates of speed, (c) consideration for the learner's interests, and (d) efforts to meet the learner's needs.

(3) The basic ingredients of an ILP are (a) concept, skill, or value statements, (b) behavioral or learning objectives, (c) individualized learning materials and activities, (d) pre-, self-, and post-assessment, and (e) quest.

*

The term, "learning activities," as used in this book, involves the following:

(1) curriculum content—what is being learned,

(2) instructional strategies—what the teacher does,

(3) learning strategies—what the learner does, and

(4) media of all types—what the teacher or student uses in instruction or learning.

LESSON 1

SUB-CONCEPT

An individualized, continuous progress curriculum allows each student to progress at his own best rate of speed commensurate with his abilities, interests, needs, and motivational patterns.

LEARNING OBJECTIVES

The learning activities in this lesson will assist you in being able to do the following:

You should be able to write a definition of an individualized, continuous progress curriculum.

You should be able to state at least three ways in which an individualized, continuous progress curriculum can provide for differences among learners.

Select from the learning activities for Lesson 1 those which suit your interests. Then progress toward achieving the learning objectives for this lesson.

LEARNING ACTIVITIES

A. Read:

Look at Your Students

Here they are ... your students for the coming year. They (thirty of them) are all seated before you. Your textbook has been given to you. Go to it! Start them all on page 1 and assign page 2 for tomorrow. By midyear they will be approximately half way through the book.

Listed below and continued on page 10 are five basic premises together with their sources which are fundamental to individualized, continuous progress education.

(1) American ideals and democratic traditions emphasize the worth, dignity, rights, and liberties of the individual, not only as sound theoretical principles but also as functioning bases for social well-being and betterment. (See sources 5, 7, and 13.)

(2) Individuals differ in abilities, personality, readiness, socio-economic backgrounds, and in the manner in which they learn. (See sources 2, 11, and 16.)

(3) Differences among students should be provided for in educational programs which promote varied activities, experiences, and materials. (See sources 4, 6, 8, and 9.)

(4) The recent "explosion of knowledge" requires that students receive instruction in concepts, facts, skills, and attitudes in greater breadth and depth than has been possible under the standard school curriculum and organizational structure. The curriculum and program must be so organized that students, through more selective processes, can progress through school programs without artificial barriers such as grade norms, age norms, and mythical averages. (See sources 3, 10, and 12.)

(5) Individuality must be preserved in the emerging, highly organized, centralized, and technologically automated society. Although innovations (particularly those connected with technological advancements) hold great promise, they also pose the threat of undermining the potential and self-determination of individuals. Properly integrated, these innovations may provide the basis for a continuous progress curriculum which promotes individuality. (See sources 1, 6, 11, 14, and 15.)

Sources

1. American Association of School Administrators, *A Climate for Individuality* (Washington, D.C.: National Education Association, 1965).

2. Anne Anasti and John P. Foley, Jr., *Differential Psychology: Individual and Group Differences and Behavior* (New York: Macmillan Company, 1949).

3. B. Frank Brown, *The Nongraded High School* (Englewood Cliffs, New Jersey: Prentice-Hall, Inc., 1963).

(Continued on page 10)

It is midyear now. So far you have managed well—you have them all on the same page. Of course, you know that Johnny could have completed the entire book by now if you had let him alone. And Mary would be at least three-fourths through. Then there is Bill—he doesn't understand what is going on. You lost him on about page ten; but each day he turns in the assignment he doesn't understand. His attitude is good (overtly) so you will social-promote him to the next grade. But Joan—she just sits. She won't even try to turn in her assignments; she didn't understand even the first page—you will have to keep her back another year... AND SO IT GOES! ANOTHER YEAR OF TREATING CHILDREN AS IF THEY WERE ALL EQUAL—EQUAL IN INTELLIGENCE, ACHIEVEMENT, READINESS, AND INTEREST.

Look at Each Student

Let's take another look at that class of thirty. Here they are:

(1) *Physical appearance*: Tall, medium, slender, fat, short, plump, with glasses, without glasses, needing glasses, with hearing aids, without hearing aids, lisps, can't pronounce "r" sounds, good looking, long hair, short hair, bulldog... YES, THERE THEY ARE!

(2) *Ability*: Brilliant, average, smart, dumb, slow learner, quick, IQ 150, IQ 70, IQ 101, creative, mechanical, verbal, nonverbal... THAT'S YOUR CLASS!

(3) *Achievement*: On grade level, above grade level, below grade level, can read text, has difficulty reading text, can't read at all, learning normally, way ahead of me... THE SAME THIRTY STUDENTS?

(4) *Interest and motivation*: Not interested, wants to be a truck driver, can't understand why it is a required course, loves it, always brings an extra something from home or the library, asks too many questions I can't answer, spends all his time drawing "pictures" of me and thinks I don't know it, smart aleck, spends her time trying to attract a boyfriend, hasn't answered a question all year... HOW ARE YOU GOING TO KEEP ALL THIRTY MOTIVATED?

(5) *Home background*: Middle class, lower class, well off, no money for lunch, good home, parents divorced, father an alcoholic, mother president of PTA, has no home, brother a black power leader, Ku Klux Klan, Catholic, Protestant, not allowed to dance, unemployed, on welfare, millionaire.... HELP! THEY ARE ALL THERE! YOUR CLASS OF THIRTY!

(Continued from page 8)

4. Commission on the Reorganization of Secondary Education, *Cardinal Principles of Secondary Education, Bulletin 35* (Washington, D.C.: U.S. Bureau of Education, 1918), p. 9.

5. *Constitution of the United States of America.*

6. *Contemporary Issues in American Education,* Consultants' Papers Prepared for Use at the White House Conference on Education (Washington, D.C.: U.S. Department of Health, Education, and Welfare, U.S. Office of Education, 1965), pp. 1-158.

7. *Declaration of Independence.*

8. Educational Policies Commission, *Education for All American Youth* (Washington, D.C.: National Education Association, 1944), pp. 15-16, 225-226.

9. _____. *The Central Purpose of American Education* (Washington, D.C.: National Education Association, 1961).

10. John I. Goodlad and Robert H. Anderson, *The Nongraded Elementary School* (New York: Harcourt, Brace, and World, Inc., 1963).

11. Nelson B. Henry (ed.), *Individualizing Instruction,* Sixty-first Yearbook of the National Society for the Study of Education, Part I (Chicago, Illinois: University of Chicago Press, 1962).

12. Edwin A. Read and John K. Crnkovic, *The Continuous Progress Plan* (Provo, Utah: Brigham Young University Press, 1963).

13. *The Report of the President's Commission on National Goals* (Englewood Cliffs, New Jersey: Prentice-Hall, Inc., 1960), pp. 1, 6-7.

14. The Rockefeller Panel Reports, "Report V—The Pursuit of Excellence: Education and the Future of America," *Prospect for America* (Garden City, New York: Doubleday and Company, 1961).

15. J. Lloyd Trump and Lois S. Karasik, *Focus on the Individual: A Leadership Responsibility* (Washington, D.C.: National Association of Secondary School Principals, 1965).

16. Leona Elizabeth Tyler, *The Psychology of Human Differences* (New York: Appleton-Century-Crofts, 1956).

If you could have your fondest wish, it would be for a curriculum planned to meet the needs of each of your students so that not one would be lost, held back, or neglected. What you need is an individualized, ungraded curriculum which would allow each student to progress according to his own ability, interests, and needs.

Teachers all over the world understand the need to provide for individual differences; yet few are successful. The primary reason given for this failure has been the lack of curriculum materials suitable for individualized programs.

The purpose of this book is to show how ILPs can make possible such a curriculum and to demonstrate ways to construct and use ILPs.

B. Do:

Self-Analysis Instrument

This learning activity is designed to facilitate an assessment of the curricular vehicles which you currently are using. Listed below are nineteen questions. Answer each question with yes or no, and add as much qualifying information as you wish. This learning activity may be conducted as a self-assessment or, if you wish, someone else can assist you by observing in your classroom.

First identify three students in one of your classes; try to select a "high," an "average," and a "low" achiever. Then respond to the following questions for each of the three students by placing a "yes" or a "no" in each of the spaces provided.

High	Av.	Low		
....	....	....	(1)	Are your students permitted to progress at their own unique rates of learning?
....	....	....	(2)	Do you test students on the content of lectures which you might present?
....	....	....	(3)	Are any of the three students which you identified for this assessment studying the same assignment?
....	....	....	(4)	Does the organization of your learning materials help students relate themes, generalizations, theories, principles, and concepts to the structure of the discipline(s) which you teach?

An ungraded, individualized, continuous progress curriculum can be justified on the following bases:

(1) fundamental political philosophy and democratic principles,

(2) educational philosophy and practice,

(3) psychological studies about individual differences, and

(4) current demands being made by society for individual excellence, creativity, and leadership.

ILP 1—Lesson 1

....   (5) Are your students given materials and techniques which encourage them to consciously and individually examine values and the processes of valuing?

....   (6) Are your students provided opportunities to select from print, non-print, and human resources for learning (media of all types)?

....   (7) Do the materials and techniques which you use help your students learn the modes and processes of investigation employed in your discipline(s)?

....   (8) Are your students given opportunities to use inquiry, discovery, and inductive procedures in their learning activities?

....   (9) Are your students provided with behavioral objectives to guide them in their learning?

....   (10) Is there always a specified sequence of subject content or learning activities which all students must follow?

....   (11) Are your students allowed to follow alternative paths in their learning sequences based on their personal interests and motivations?

....   (12) Have you incorporated games and/or simulation techniques and materials into the learning activities employed by your students?

....   (13) Are your students provided opportunities to select from learning materials aimed at a variety of difficulty levels?

....   (14) Are texts which are written at different reading difficulty levels available to your students?

....   (15) Do the learning materials provided for your students contain contents which are discussed at differing depths of sophistication or abstractness?

Additional background information in the theory and techniques of curriculum construction for realism, relevance, and individualization is available in the following sources:

Books

1. David W. Beggs, III, and Edward G. Buffie (eds.), *Independent Study: Bold New Venture* (Bloomington: Indiana University Press, 1965), 236 pp.

2. B. Frank Brown, *Education by Appointment: New Approaches to Independent Study* (West Nyack, New York: Parker Publishing Company, Inc., 1968), 175 pp.

3. Jerome S. Bruner, *The Process of Education* (Cambridge, Massachusetts: Harvard University Press, 1960), 97 pp.

4. Ronald C. Doll (ed.), *Individualizing Instruction,* 1964 Yearbook of the Association for Supervision and Curriculum Development (Washington, D.C.: The Association, 1964), 174 pp.

5. Thorwald Esbensen, *Working with Individualized Instruction: The Duluth Experience* (Palo Alto, California: Fearon Publishers, 1968), 122 pp.

6. John I. Goodlad, *School, Curriculum, and the Individual* (Waltham, Massachusetts: Blaisdell Publishing Company, 1966), 259 pp.

7. Robert F. Mager, *Developing Attitude Toward Learning* (Palo Alto, California: Fearon Publishers, 1968), 104 pp.

8. Don H. Parker, *Schooling for Individual Excellence* (New York: Thomas Nelson & Sons, 1964), 285 pp.

Films

1. *Charlie and the Golden Hamster.* 13 min., 16mm, sound, color. /I/D/E/A/ Informational Services Division, Post Office Box 446, Melbourne, Florida, 32901.

2. *The Improbable Form of Master Sturm.* 13 min., 16mm, sound, color. /I/D/E/A/ Informational Services Division, Post Office Box 446, Melbourne, Florida, 32901.

3. *Make a Mighty Reach.* 45 min., 16mm, sound, color. /I/D/E/A/ Informational Services Division, Post Office Box 446, Melbourne, Florida, 32901, 1967.

4. *Why Man Creates.* 25 min., 16mm, sound, color. Pyramid Film Producers, Box 1048, Santa Monica, California, 90406, 1968. (Also available in Super 8mm with sound.)

.... (16) Do the learning materials provided for your students contain topics which are discussed from opposing or divergent points of view?

.... (17) Does your curricular vehicle provide for individual differences in student self-initiative?

.... (18) Does your curricular vehicle provide for individual differences in student self-direction?

.... (19) Does your curricular vehicle help students to increasingly value self-responsibility?

How did you do? If you have an individualized, continuous progress program, your answers for each question for each of the three students you identified earlier may be as follows: (1) yes, (2) no, (3) no, (4) yes, (5) yes, (6) yes, (7) yes, (8) yes, (9) yes, (10) no, (11) yes, (12) yes, (13) yes, (14) yes, (15) yes, (16) yes, (17) yes, (18) yes, and (19) yes. Of course, you may have had to qualify some of your answers; but, without using some kind of an ILP design it would be almost impossible to provide for all of the kinds of individualization suggested by the above questions.

CHECK YOUR PROGRESS

(1) What is an individualized, continuous progress curriculum?
(2) Why is such an individualized curriculum needed?
(3) Question 2 above asks for a behavior which is related to, although not identical with, the behavior desired in the second learning objective for this lesson. Be sure you re-read the objectives as a part of checking your own progress.

SELF-TEST KEY

(1) An individualized, continuous progress curriculum is one which has been ungraded in such a way that each student can, individually, move through the content of the curriculum at his own pace commensurate with his own abilities, interests, and needs.
(2) An individualized, continuous progress curriculum is needed because each person is so different that it is educationally unsound to assume that all students in a class are ever at any one common point in learning.
(3) Have you achieved the second learning objective for this lesson?

If you are satisfied with your achievement of the objectives for Lesson 1, move ahead to Lesson 2. If the results of the self-test indicate that you need greater depth, you may wish to review or use more extensively some of the sources suggested on the opposite page.

LESSON 2

SUB-CONCEPT

Individualized instruction and learning can occur when the curriculum and the materials and activities are organized for self-pacing through ILPs.

LEARNING OBJECTIVE

You should be able to list the basic ingredients found in an ILP.

Four learning activities are provided in this lesson. Begin by thinking about the conditions under which you learn best when you are not going to school. (Let's face it—much of our best learning goes on outside of school.) Isn't learning much more efficient for you when you have clearly in mind where you are going (your objective), how you will get there (your route and strategy), and how you will know when you have reached your goal (your evaluation of goal attainment)? Therefore, look over all of the suggested learning activities before choosing to do one or more of them. Use the learning objective we provided; embellish it with your own relevance and meaning.

LEARNING ACTIVITIES

A. Read:

The Ingredients of an ILP

The need for continuous progress has been identified and substantiated in the preceding pages. Most teachers will agree that selective instruction based on individual learning ability and style should replace our presently used "batch" process. Teaching for the so-called average student in group-paced instruction results in too many students becoming in-school or out-of-school dropouts. Both fast and slow learners lack stimulation in this type of situation. In addition, slow learners continually find themselves "in over their heads" in their instructional program. But, what can be done about the problem *now*? How can we respond to the obvious need for continuous educational progress, while saddled with the curricular materials which are presently available? We know full well that the vast majority of these materials were designed to make group-paced instruction workable, regardless of what we know about how learning occurs.

The practical implementation of continuous educational progress necessitates a frontal assault on the curriculum. Programmed learning, whether in book form or computerized, is a partial answer to achieving more flexible curricula. This is

particularly true in content areas which require detailed, repetitive instruction. Random retrieval systems, utilizing tape decks and dial access, are still another partial answer. Educational or instructional television is another component of more flexible curricula, especially when a documentary approach to programming is utilized. However, any of these systems, when used solely for group instruction, serve only to perpetuate the same problems that have been with us ever since the first teacher expected two or more students to learn the same thing in the same amount of time using the same curricular materials.

A flexible curriculum does not necessitate discarding the individual elements which make up the curriculum now in use. Rather, the curriculum must be restructured. Content and process, as prescribed in media such as textbooks, films, and programmed materials, must be reorganized so as to be available to students in a form which will facilitate rather than hinder self-paced learning. Concept, skill, and value statements can serve as focal points of such reorganization; units, modules, or packages of learning (or whatever other name one wishes to employ) can then be prepared for use by individual students or small learning teams.

We have employed the term, Individualized Learning Package, for such a concept-, skill-, or value-centered, behaviorally-oriented, self-paced unit. The ILP has been organized around the following five curricular ingredients:

(1) *Concepts.*—ILPs should be centered around learnable ideas or concepts, skills, and values. Jerome Bruner, Harvard psychologist, has pointed out the importance of teaching specific topics in relation to the fundamental structure of a field of knowledge. By relating what is learned to such a structure, learning becomes more economical, rewarding, usable, and readily retained. Skills in routine operations and knowledge of facts, rather than being ends in themselves, serve as the learner's entree to comprehension of concepts and ideas. By preparing ILPs which are concept-centered, such skills and facts can be organized into meaningful patterns. Specialized inquiry processes also can be related to general principles through ILPs.

(2) *Behavioral or learning objectives.*—Good teachers have always communicated to their students the levels of performance and achievement expected at evaluation time, but often this has been accomplished orally and informally. In individualized instruction, students break out of the curricular lockstep and progress at their own best rates, working toward their learning objectives. Although student learning teams may be formed, consisting of perhaps two to six students, the membership of such teams fluctuates. On the other hand, one student might be studying completely different materials, at a given point in time, than any other student, and

thus a learning team could not be formed. Therefore, in individualized instruction it is necessary for teachers to formalize learning objectives in writing, and to include these objectives in each ILP.

(3) *Individualized learning materials and activities.*—Students do learn in different ways; each student has his own unique learning skills or "styles" which may be categorized as primarily visual (reading), aural (listening), or physical (doing things). Of course, most people find more than one of these styles comfortable or useful at different times. In order to provide for such variability, alternative media and activities of all types for achieving learning objectives should be suggested to the student in the ILP. Provision should be made for student use of a wide variety of commercially prepared visual materials such as selections from textbooks and other books, programmed materials, filmstrips, and 35mm slides; aural materials such as tapes and other recordings; physical activities such as model building, experiments, and role-playing; and combinations such as audiovisual films, small group discussions, field studies, and interviews. Teacher-prepared material also may be included. The more extensive the diversification of materials and methodologies of instruction in the ILP, the greater may be the utility of the package.

(4) *Pre-, self-, and post-assessment.*—The combination of pre- and post-assessment by the teacher serves to measure learning growth which cannot be measured by post-assessment alone. In addition, pre-assessment permits the teacher and student to determine which learning objectives might already have been achieved, so that the student is able to invest his time wisely in areas in which he is weak. Self-assessment serves to help the student monitor his own progress. When the student has achieved one objective, he can go on to the next one. When the results of self-assessment indicate to him that he is ready for teacher assessment, he can request post-assessment. Directions to the student to contact the teacher for pre- and post-assessment should be built into the student's copy of the ILP.

(5) *Quest.*—Although ILPs provide structure for each student's learning experiences, decisions inherent in using ILPs encourage the development of self-initiative and self-direction. However, even greater self-initiating and self-directing experience should be made available to every student. ILPs should include opportunities for quest—for enrichment study, whether in breadth or in depth. Problem statements might be included so that the student is stimulated to define a problem for quest study, carry out his research, and achieve some level of resolution of the problem which he has chosen. The student also should be encouraged through quest to investigate topics of his own creation.

The following format is suitable for writing a single lesson in an ILP:

Lesson # ....

Lesson Title ....

(1) Component Concept, Skill, or Value:* ....
....

(2) Learning Objective(s): ....
....

(3) Learning Activities:
    (a) ....
    (b) ....
    (c) ....
    (d) ....
    (e) ....

(4) Self-Evaluation: ....
....

(5) Quest:** ....
....

*Verbalization of the component concept, skill, or value may be omitted in the student's copy of the ILP lesson when a "guided discovery" approach is used.

**Quest suggestions may be placed in each lesson or at the end of a series of lessons making up an ILP.

B. Do:

ILP Format

Examine the organization and contents of the ILP lessons in this book. Compare these to the sample format (opposite page) for writing ILP lessons. Which basic ingredients of an ILP are accounted for within a single lesson? Which ingredients of an ILP are not included? How could you include the five basic ingredients of an ILP in an audio system for young children who are not yet able to follow a written ILP?

C. Select:

Philip G. Kapfer, "Practical Approaches to Individualizing Instruction," *Educational Screen and Audiovisual Guide,* XLVII (May, 1968), 14-16.

_____ and Gardner Swenson, "Individualizing Instruction for Self-Paced Learning," *The Clearing House,* XLII (March, 1968), 405-410.

Glen F. Ovard, "A Model for Developing an Individualized Continuous Progress Curriculum Unit Emphasizing Concepts and Behavioral Objectives" (Provo, Utah: Education Experimental Programs, Brigham Young University, 1967), 19 pp. (Mimeo.)

D. Do:

Library Research

Use the *Education Index* to find recent periodical sources on nongrading, individual differences, individual instruction, or any other entry word topics of interest to you that relate to this ILP lesson.

CHECK YOUR PROGRESS

Can you recall and list the five basic ingredients of Individualized Learning Packages?

SELF-TEST KEY

The five basic ingredients of Individualized Learning Packages are (1) concepts, skills, and/or values, (2) behavioral or learning objectives, (3) individualized learning materials and activities, (4) pre-, self-, and post-assessment methods, and (5) quest.

If you could not recall the essential ingredients of an ILP, review this lesson. If you had difficulty understanding what these ingredients mean in relation to the instructional design, ILP 8 may help you to relate these ingredients to what the teacher and the students do in a continuous progress program. If you feel ready, the post-test covering both lessons in ILP 1 comes next.

As pointed out at the beginning of this ILP, the post-test and post-test answers would not usually be placed in the student's copy of an ILP. The post-test or assessment is the teacher's evaluation of the progress of the learner. Success or failure determines what guidance or direction the teacher should then give the student. In performing this task, the teacher is acting in the role of diagnostician and prescriber—as a consultant to learning.

*

POST-TEST FOR ILP 1

Now that you have completed the activities for Lessons 1 and 2 and have checked your degree of knowledge growth, you are ready for the post-test covering the entire ILP.

(1) Write a definition of an individualized, continuous progress curriculum.

(2) Describe at least three ways in which such a curriculum can help to solve problems related to effectively meeting individual differences among students.

(3) List five basic ingredients of an ILP.

ILP 1—Follow-up

Complete the post-test for ILP 1 (opposite page). After finishing the post-test, you have three options: (1) you may choose to engage in quest activities such as those which follow, (2) you may proceed to ILP 2 entitled "What Will Be Learned?" or (3) you may proceed to one of the other ILPs in this book according to your interests and readiness. If you choose quest activities, you are expanding the depth or breadth of your understanding of the concepts you explored in ILP 1. If you choose to proceed to ILP 2 instead of engaging in quest, you are increasing your rate of progress through this book. If you choose to personalize your learning sequence by doing other ILPs before ILP 2, you may be listening to a "different drummer":

> *If a man does not keep pace with his companions,*
> *Perhaps it is because he hears a different drummer.*
> *Let him step to the music which he hears,*
> *However measured or far away.*
>
> *Henry David Thoreau*

POST-TEST KEY FOR ILP 1

(1) An individualized, continuous progress curriculum is an ungraded program which allows the learner to proceed through the concepts, skills, and values to be learned at his own rate of speed commensurate with his abilities, interests, needs, and motivational patterns.

(2) An individualized, continuous progress curriculum provides for student differences through (a) individual selection of learning materials, (b) learner-regulated rates of speed, (c) consideration for the learner's interests, and (d) efforts to meet the learner's needs.

(3) The basic ingredients of an ILP are (a) concept, skill, or value statements, (b) behavioral or learning objectives, (c) individualized learning materials and activities, (d) pre-, self-, and post-assessment, and (e) quest.

*

Quest provides the learner with choices for expansion in his knowledge, either in the content just studied in an ILP or in related areas. Quest is the student's choice—even the choice *not* to participate in quest. In quest, the teacher serves as a consultant to learning rather than the director of it. Whenever a teacher is tempted to *require* selection of a particular quest topic by his students, he should consider placing that topic in the learning activities section of the ILP rather than in the quest section. In summary, quest might well serve as a barometer of student interest and of the relevance of a particular subject to student needs.

QUEST

A. Would you like to investigate individualization further? Some entry words into the professional literature that you might use are (1) continuous progress curriculum, (2) ungraded curriculum, and (3) learning packages.

B. How do the curricular ingredients of ILPs differ from the ingredients of (1) UNIPACs, (2) the University of Pittsburgh's Individually Prescribed Instruction (IPI), (3) the Teaching-Learning Units (TLUs) produced by the American Institutes for Research, (4) Nova's Learning Activity Packages (LAPs), and (5) Duluth's Student Learning Contracts (SLCs)?

C. Are there any other topics in which you have become interested as a result of your study of ILP 1? Quest is your opportunity for choice. If you are using this book with the assistance of an instructor, he should know what quest topic you chose to study so that he can be available for consultation should you desire it.

PART II: CURRICULAR COMPONENTS
HERE ARE THE PIECES!

ILP 2

WHAT WILL BE LEARNED?

Concept, Skill and Value Statements

CONCEPT

The knowledge or content to be learned can be structured according to concepts, skills, and values (the learnable ideas, skills, and attitudes).

SUB-CONCEPTS

Identifying and writing the major concepts, skills, and values to be learned is the first step in creating an ILP.

Major concepts, skills, and values may be divided into sub-concepts, sub-skills, and sub-values which are also called "component parts." ("Component parts" may be thought of as the sub-parts which are necessary for an understanding of the whole.)

Statements of the component parts of concepts, skills, and values, written at the level of the learner, define and clarify the scope of the curricular content to be covered in an ILP.

LEARNING OBJECTIVES

When given a list of ten items, you should be able to identify all items by indicating whether they are concepts, skills, or values.

You should be able to write major concept, skill, and value statements in a subject area of interest to you.

This ILP is concerned with *how* to write concept, skill, and value statements at the level of a given learner or group of learners. In other words, this ILP is concerned primarily with *how* concepts, skills, and values are built into learning packages rather than with the theory justifying *why* concepts, skills, and values are used in the structure of knowledge. We have purposely oversimplified the "structure of knowledge theory" (or "concept-centered learning theory") so that we can demonstrate the use of ideas, skills, and attitudes in reordering curricular content into learning packages.

*

PRE-TEST FOR ILP 2

(1) Identify each item in the list of concepts, skills, and values below by placing C, S, or V in the spaces provided (100 percent accuracy is required).

- ....(a) In our economic system, certain segments of the population do not contribute to the G.N.P.
- ....(b) We should love our country.
- ....(c) Dribble the ball ten times.
- ....(d) Rioting and disrespect for law and order are bad for our country.
- ....(e) Shoot a marble across the ring.
- ....(f) Reading books should be a pleasant experience.
- ....(g) The schwa is a symbol "ə" representing a softened vowel sound.
- ....(h) Sew a button hole.
- ....(i) A lever is a simple machine that has three classes.
- ....(j) Draw an object in which the principle of perspective is represented.

(2) Choose a subject area and learning level of interest to you. Determine and write statements for one major idea in each of the following categories: (a) concept, (b) skill, and (c) value.

(3) Using the major concept, skill, and value statements developed in #2 above, analyze and state in simple, complete form the component parts necessary for an understanding of each major idea.

*

From the standpoint of ILP form, it should be noted that the pre-test may be packaged equally well in the student's part of the ILP rather than in the teacher's materials. However, one would seldom (and only for mature, responsible, self-directed students) put the pre-test answers in the student's part of the ILP.

ILP 2—Preliminaries

Using the major concept, skill, and value statements that you just developed, you should be able to analyze and state in writing the component parts of each. Both the major ideas and the component parts should be stated in simple, complete form at the desired learning level.

We have chosen to structure our ILPs around the question, "What is to be learned?" Only later do we ask the question, "What behavior (learning objective) is expected of the learner in relation to what is being learned?" There are some consultants in the area of the development of learning packages, however, who believe that the objectives for learning should be the central point around which the learning package is structured. If you prefer the latter approach, we suggest that you cycle yourself directly to ILP 3 (in which the topic of learning objectives is dealt with in detail) and then return to ILP 2. We suggest the return to ILP 2 in any case because we believe that behavior must be in relation to something. That something is the content of ILP 2—the concepts, skills, and values to be learned.

Irrespective of the sequence in which you decide to do the ILPs in this book, the next order of business within ILP 2 is the pre-test (opposite page). When you have completed the test, ask your instructor for assistance in checking your responses and in selecting the lessons or learning activities from ILP 2 (if any are needed) which will best fortify the weak spots in your understanding of the concepts in this ILP. If you are using this book as a lone learner, make your own decisions based on the information contained in the pre-test key on the next page.

PRE-TEST KEY FOR ILP 2

(1)   (a) C   (c) S   (e) S   (g) C   (i) C
            (b) V   (d) V   (f) V   (h) S   (j) S

(2)   Use the following criteria for judging your responses to item #2 on the pre-test:

        (a)   Are the major ideas stated simply and completely?
        (b)   Are they clearly understandable?
        (c)   Are they written at the language level of the proposed learner?

       Also try comparing the concept, skill, and value statements you wrote with the examples in this ILP. Notice that the examples are written in the form of fairly simple statements rather than as questions, exclamations, or imperatives.

(3)   Apply the criteria given in #2 above to the statements of component parts. Then check each component to determine if each is a logical part of the major concept (or skill or value). Be sure, in each case, that all component parts are a *part of* the major idea rather than separate ideas at the same level. In other words, you must decide whether all of the component parts of each major idea belong in a single ILP or whether some belong logically in other ILPs.

       You also might find it helpful to try out the component parts of each major idea on members of your family or some other group. Note and analyze the diversity of understanding of each person with regard to each component part. You should be able to account for reasonable differences in levels of concept formation, skill development, and value definition while still being confident that each set of component parts belongs in a single ILP.

*

Each ILP lesson focuses on one or more component parts of the major concept, skill, or value to be learned in a particular ILP. In each lesson, the component part or parts are developed together with related objectives, learning activities, and the necessary instructions. An ILP may contain from one to several lessons, the exact number being dependent on whatever is required to present adequately all of the component parts of the major idea, skill, or value.

LESSON 1

SUB-CONCEPT

Identifying and writing the major concepts, skills, and values to be learned is the first step in creating an ILP.

LEARNING OBJECTIVES

When given a list of ten items, you should be able to identify all items by indicating whether they are concepts, skills, or values.

You should be able to write major concept, skill, and value statements in a subject area of interest to you.

You are now ready to learn how to identify and write concept, skill, and value statements for ILPs. You may choose from the four learning activities which follow in order to build your understanding and background sufficiently to achieve the learning objectives for this lesson.

LEARNING ACTIVITIES

A. Read:

Choosing an Idea for an ILP

What is important?—By now everyone has heard of the "knowledge explosion." New knowledge is being discovered at a rate so rapid that the total amount of existing knowledge doubles every 7.2 years. Soon the total amount of all existing knowledge will double every five years.

The dilemma of the teacher with regard to this problem is "How can I include in my classes all the *new* knowledge relating to my teaching area when I am not able to get through the present textbook as it is?" As a result, teachers of every subject must ask themselves, "What is really important?" and "Why should a student learn *this* rather than something else?" Obviously, value judgments must be made about *what* is to be learned.

Some educators have tried to solve the knowledge explosion problem by concentrating on process alone—that is, on the "how" of knowledge and learning. However, we believe that the "what" of learning is also significant. Thus, the initial

The learning activities in ILPs are designed to help the learner arrive at expected behaviors. Because individuals are different, a variety of activities leading to the same goal should be included in each ILP lesson. By this means, individual differences can be provided for through various modes of learning. The activities can be designed (1) so that complete choice is possible, (2) so that some activities are required while some are elective, or (3) so that all activities are required. The last design, which involves the least flexibility, would be used only occasionally in order to meet special circumstances.

task of the ILP writer is to sort, cut, throw away, and find the relevant. When this has been done, the ILP can be organized for effective in-school learning of in-life behaviors.

About concepts, skills, and values.—During recent decades, scholars in the area of the structure of knowledge have repeatedly debated the question of ways in which knowledge can be most usefully categorized for teaching and learning purposes. This debate has resulted, among other things, in the publication of the well-known *Taxonomy of Educational Objectives* in the cognitive and affective domains (1956 and 1964). The development of a third domain, the psychomotor, has been published in preliminary form (1966) and is still under revision.

Basically, these three domains or categories of human learning correspond to the terms "concepts," "values," and "skills" which we have chosen to use in this book. Although there are many advantages to the use of such classification schemes, there are also some problems involved. And you, as a potential user of such schemes, should be aware of both the positive and negative aspects.

The first of these problems involves the fact that while the division of knowledge into the three categories just mentioned is neat and useful, it is also oversimplified and therefore somewhat inaccurate. For example, concept, skill, and value learnings are not really as separate and distinct as one might think or wish. In fact, recent studies have indicated that all affective domain ideas (values) and goals are based upon and probably inseparable from cognitive knowledge. Of course, some behaviors which we infer to be value-related frequently were learned originally through some process of conditioning. When we attempt to educate (as opposed to train) in the area of values, we are attempting to provide a conceptual basis for value judgments.

It has long been established that man must choose between alternatives. Yet little has been said about the character of his choices. Choices imply alternatives. Choosing from among alternatives implies values. One alternative may be good for a person while another alternative may be bad. The values which we hold are those concepts of the desirable which influence our choices among the available means, modes, and ends of action. Thus, when alternatives are present, one chooses according to values—that is, according to one's concept of the desirable. The focusing of ILPs on values or value statements affords the learner structured opportunities to practice behaviors related to making choices and decisions.

Stated more completely, concept, skill, and value learning all require conceptualization. For example, the obvious concentration of a young child as he directs a spoonful of food to his mouth eventually gives way to a nearly automatic process which is conducted with very little thought. Thus, even psychomotor skills, which subsequently become almost kinesthetic in character, initially require considerable mental effort or conceptualization.

A second problem relates to the discrepancy which sometimes exists between what

the learner is able to *verbalize* concerning a concept and what his actual *conceptualization* really consists of. A concept frequently is thought of as a complete and meaningful idea that is found in the mind of a person. When we write a concept statement in order to describe such conceptualization, we assume that the verbal statement accurately represents the mental image of the phenomena (objects, processes, and consequences) which the learner experiences. The trap that we then too frequently fall into is that we equate a learner's verbalization of a concept with his conceptualization, when the two may not, in fact, be the same. In other words, until the learner has adequately experienced the phenomena from which the concept statement was derived, conceptualization cannot occur.

To summarize thus far and to clarify our terminology, we recognize that concepts involve all three domains—cognitive, psychomotor, and affective. When we use the word "concept" in an ILP, however, we mean primarily the "cognitive domain." When we use the word "skill," we mean primarily the "psychomotor domain." And when the word "value" is used, we are referring to the "affective domain." The words "concepts," "skills," and "values" were chosen rather than possibly more precise terms simply in order to communicate better with readers who have had little previous experience with the more technical terminology.

Why write concepts, skills, and values in the form of statements?—Let us consider why we believe it is essential to use sentences rather than single words to describe the concepts, skills, and values around which ILPs can be built. A concept is a subjective mental image of what a person has perceived through his senses. At the concrete level, a concept may be the mental image of an object or event such as a "chair," a "dental appointment," or "batting a ball." At the more abstract level, a concept is the mental image of a synthesis of a number of conclusions of a person which are based on experiences related to the concept. Illustrations of generally more complex concepts might include "commutative property," "gravitational force," "love," and "loyalty."

Both simple and complex concepts, when recalled as single words, take on a variety of meanings. For example, even comparatively ordinary words such as "race," "game," and "car" create different mental images in the mind of each student. Concepts based on such words communicate better if written in sentences.

Using a series of different examples, let us look again at what happens when single words are used to try to convey concepts:

(1) *Table.*—What is a table to a five year old child? a chemistry student? a gambler? a water conservationist?

(2) *Patriotism.*—What is patriotism to a first grade student? a junior high student? a twelfth grade student in American government? a communist? a draft card burner?

(3) *Disadvantaged.*—What does "disadvantaged" mean to the millionaire? the person earning under $3,000 per year? the hippie? the ghetto Negro? the social worker? the middle class Caucasian?

To summarize, concepts are subjective to each person based on unique sets of individual experiences. Therefore, it is critical to the learning process that the concepts to be learned be explicitly defined. One of the best ways in which concepts (or skills or values) can convey the intended meaning is to state them in simple, concise sentences.

B. Do:

Writing and Comparing Concept Statements

Using the last three sample concepts discussed in Learning Activity A above (namely "table," "patriotism," and "disadvantaged"), write one or more concept statements for each word. Compare your written statements with the ones we have listed below. Does the need for concept, skill, and value statements rather than single-word concepts become evident after such a comparison?

(1) A table is used for eating (pre-school level).

(2) A periodic table is a device for organizing the chemical elements (secondary level).

(3) The water table is affected by the amount of rain or snow which falls (water engineer, farmer).

(4) Patriotism is pledging allegiance to your country (primary level).

(5) Dying a hero's death is the highest form of patriotism (junior high school level).

(6) Acting as a responsible citizen is patriotism in action (secondary level).

(7) To be disadvantaged is to be without domestic help and gardening service (the very rich).

(8) According to government classification, the "poor" are the disadvantaged earning under $3,000 per year (the social worker).

(9) To be disadvantaged is having less than the "Joneses" (middle class Caucasian).

By placing the above ideas within concept statements, each idea has been given sufficient concreteness and clarification to be useful for development into ILPs at varying learning levels.

Additional information on concept learning may be found in the following sources:

Books

1. Robert M. Gagné, *The Conditions of Learning* (New York: Holt, Rinehart and Winston, Inc., 1965), 308 pp.

2. Robert Glaser, "Concept Learning and Concept Teaching," *Learning Research and School Subjects,* eds. R. Gagné and W.J. Gephart (Itasca, Illinois: F.E. Peacock Publishers, 1968), pp. 1-38.

3. Anatol Pikas, *Abstraction and Concept Formation* (Cambridge, Massachusetts: Harvard University Press, 1966), 303 pp.

C. Select:

Books

1. Benjamin S. Bloom (ed.), *Taxonomy of Educational Objectives, Handbook I: Cognitive Domain* (New York: David McKay Company, Inc., 1956), 207 pp.

2. David R. Krathwohl, Benjamin S. Bloom, and Bertram B. Masia, *Taxonomy of Educational Objectives, Handbook II: Affective Domain* (New York: David McKay Company, Inc., 1964), 196 pp.

3. Asahel D. Woodruff, *Basic Concepts of Teaching* (San Francisco: Chandler Publishing Company, 1961), 238 pp. See especially Chapters 7 and 8.

Periodical

Elizabeth Jane Simpson, "The Classification of Educational Objectives, Psychomotor Domain," *Illinois Teacher of Home Economics,* X (Winter, 1966-67), 110-144.

Audiotape

Susan M. Markle and P.W. Tiemann, *Really Understanding Concepts* (Chicago, Illinois: Tiemann Associates, 1969), audiotape-slide materials with accompanying program book.

D. Do:

Identifying and Developing Concept Statements

Identify several concepts from your teaching level and field. Develop a concept statement for each. In a small group of your peers, discuss and evaluate the statements written by each person.

E. Read:

Sample Concept, Skill, and Value Statements

The following concept, skill, and value statements illustrate the type of major ideas that serve as effective foci for ILPs.

Concepts

1. The structure of the tepee was well suited to the life of the Plains Indians (intermediate level, social science).

2. Three colors, called primary colors, can be mixed in certain ways to make three other colors, called binary colors (primary level, art).

3. Magnets are objects which have a force that is an important source of power (primary level, science).

4. The use of guide words promotes efficiency in dictionary usage (intermediate level, language arts).

Skills

1. Recognize and pronounce the "wh" when seen in a word (primary level, phonics).

2. Write a composite sequence of the following five previously learned forms of poetic writing: haiku, tanka, Spencerian sonnet, ballad, and triolet (senior high school level, English).

3. Tell time to the hour (primary level, mathematics).

4. Advance speed in typing from 55 g.w.p.m. to 60 g.w.p.m. (secondary level, typing).

Values

1. Patriotism is saluting the flag (primary level, social science). (Another writer of an ILP might take the same basic idea but state it in a different context, such as "Patriotism is marching in a parade.")

2. Black is beautiful (all levels, social science).

3. Poetry is enjoyable (all levels, language arts).

4. The scientific know-how that created atomic power is not responsible for war (secondary level, science).

As already noted, the "Check Your Progress" section of each ILP is a self-test. Self-tests are designed to sample learning growth in relation to stated learning objectives. Such a sampling process could involve nearly any type of assessment so long as growth toward one or more specified objectives is actually being measured. In the self-test for Lesson 1 of ILP 2 (opposite page), the behavior change or learning increment which is being sampled is the ability to create satisfactory concept, skill, and value statements. This type of sampling obviously encompasses the two learning objectives identified for the lesson.

CHECK YOUR PROGRESS

Formulate in writing a major concept statement around which you could build an ILP appropriate to your teaching level and field. Do the same in the areas of skills and values.

SELF-TEST KEY

There can be no single "key" to the above self-test item, as each person's major concept, skill, and value statements will be different. The following criteria, however, will serve as your basis for judging the quality or usefulness of the statements which you wrote:

(1) Is each concept (or skill or value) stated simply and completely?
(2) Is each clearly understandable?
(3) Is each written at the language level of the proposed learner?

If you have difficulty evaluating your own achievement, ask your instructor (where possible) or a peer to render an opinion.

When you feel that you have satisfactorily achieved the learning objectives specified for Lesson 1, you are ready to go on to another lesson or ILP. You probably (although not necessarily) will wish to go to Lesson 2 in this ILP, which deals with the analysis of major concepts, skills, and values into their component parts.

Frequently there will be a one-to-one relationship between the number of sub-concepts (or sub-skills or sub-values) and the number of learning objectives in an ILP lesson. However, this relationship is not mandatory. You will note in Lesson 2, for example, that there are two sub-concepts and only one learning objective. In Lesson 2, the sub-concepts happen to be discrete while the learning objective and activities that relate to the first sub-concept relate equally to the second. The opposite relationship also sometimes exists between the number of sub-concepts and learning objectives. Sometimes two or more objectives are needed to fully cover a behavior suggested by a given sub-concept. Your best guide in matching sub-concepts and learning objectives is a flexible response to the question, "What will best facilitate learning?"

One further word on the topic of ILP form and content—by this time you will have noted that the sub-concepts and learning objectives which are related to each other are usually restated at the beginning of each lesson. This procedure serves to reinforce the ideas to be learned and also reminds the learner of the expected behavior or behaviors in relation to the component ideas.

LESSON 2

SUB-CONCEPTS

Major concepts, skills, and values may be divided into sub-concepts, sub-skills, and sub-values which are also called "component parts." ("Component parts" may be thought of as the sub-parts which are necessary for an understanding of the whole.)

Statements of the component parts of concepts, skills, and values, written at the level of the learner, define and clarify the scope of the curricular content to be covered in an ILP.

LEARNING OBJECTIVE

Using the major concept, skill, and value statements developed in Lesson 1, you should be able to analyze and state in writing the component parts of each. Both the major ideas and the component parts should be stated in simple, complete form at the desired learning level.

You are now ready to start on the learning activities which will help you understand and write the component parts of major concepts, skills, and values. Do as many of the following activities as are necessary for you to learn how (1) to analyze into component parts the major concept, skill, and value statements which you wrote in Lesson 1 of this ILP, and (2) to make those major ideas and their component parts meaningful to a learner for whom you might design an ILP.

LEARNING ACTIVITIES

A. Read:

Identifying the Sub-Concepts (or Component Parts) of a Concept

The following set of procedural steps is useful in identifying and stating the sub-concepts for an ILP.

1. Identify the key words (or phrases) in the major idea or concept.

2. Write statements for each key word (or phrase) that you identified in #1.

3. Be sure the sub-concept statements, when synthesized, result in the major concept. If they do not, add sub-concepts which seem to supply missing links. As a reverse checking procedure, then determine whether the original concept statement needs the addition of one or more key words which relate to the added sub-concepts.

4. Decide, based on the breadth and depth of coverage desired, whether all or only some of the sub-concepts that you identified will be used in the ILP being constructed.

5. Put the statements in sequence based on whatever criteria might apply, such as (a) least difficult to most difficult, (b) dependency factors, (c) groupings based on typical treatment in available media, etc.

In the learning activities in the remainder of this lesson, you will find samples of concepts and sub-concepts. Some of the examples are complete (in terms of all possible components being present) and some are not. Use the above five steps as you study the samples in order to develop the essential skill of concept analysis.

B. Read:

A Curricular Frame of Reference for the Component Parts of Major Concepts, Skills, or Values

The ILP is neither a teaching unit, a resource unit, nor a course of study. It is a flexible and individualized learning guide which is focused, at the most discrete level, on the component parts of a major concept, skill, or value. As such, however, it conforms easily to the framework of "courses" and "units" as these are commonly and currently defined.

Most educators have been trained to view the curriculum in major segments of learning or in major time blocks. This view of the curriculum tends to focus on "courses of study" and, within each course, on "units of work." The course of study is usually a full year or at least a semester in length and includes several units of work. A unit often requires from two to six weeks for completion and includes a number of major ideas. Because a typical ILP focuses on only one major idea, a unit will consist of several ILPs.

The component parts of each major concept, skill, or value are the subdivisions of the major idea. Each component part may be placed in a separate lesson, or a combination of two or more component parts may be used in a single lesson. In Figure 1 below, the component parts are shown within the context of a total course of study.

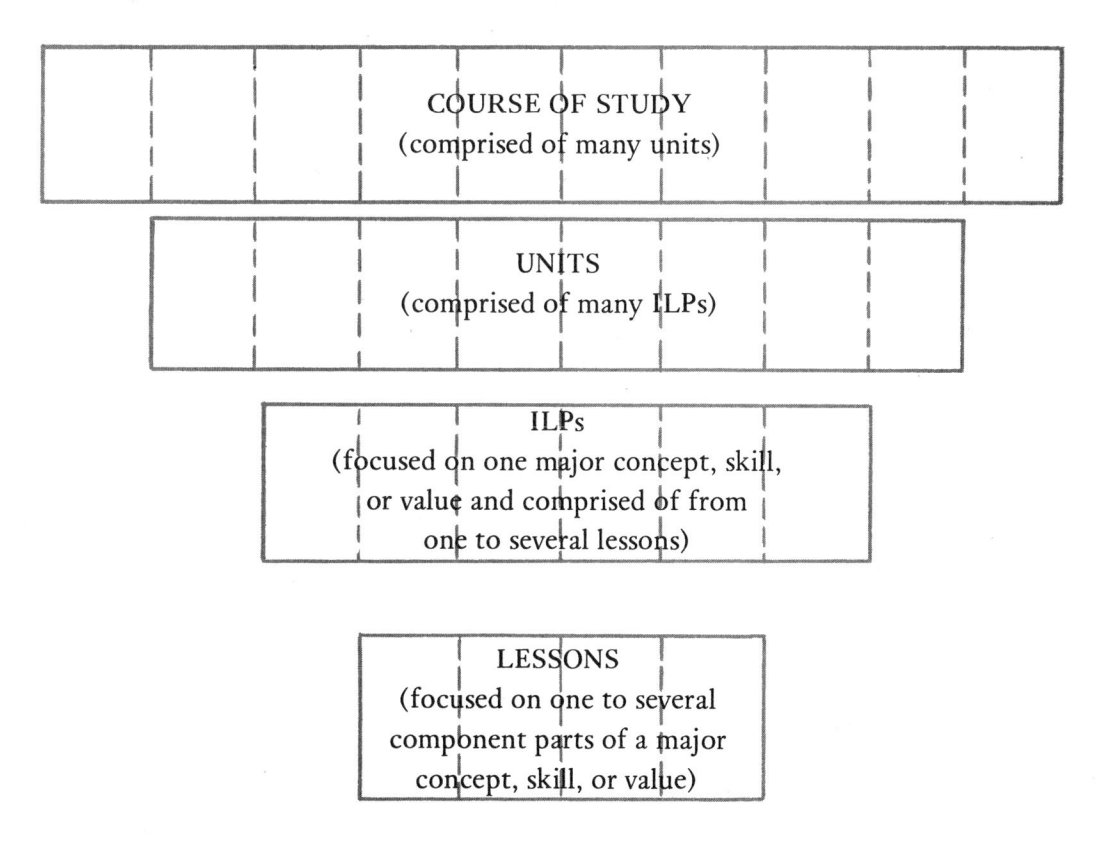

```
┌─────────────────────────────────────────────────┐
│              COURSE OF STUDY                    │
│           (comprised of many units)             │
└─────────────────────────────────────────────────┘
    ┌─────────────────────────────────────┐
    │               UNITS                 │
    │       (comprised of many ILPs)      │
    └─────────────────────────────────────┘
         ┌───────────────────────────┐
         │            ILPs           │
         │ (focused on one major concept, skill, │
         │   or value and comprised of from      │
         │        one to several lessons)        │
         └───────────────────────────┘
              ┌──────────────────────┐
              │       LESSONS        │
              │ (focused on one to several │
              │  component parts of a major │
              │   concept, skill, or value) │
              └──────────────────────┘
```

Figure 1—*The component parts of a major concept, skill, or value in relation to a total course of study.*

In Lesson 1 of this ILP, the point was made that major concepts, skills, and values should be stated in the form of sentences rather than as single words. The same is also true of the *component* concepts, skills, and values. In the examples of concepts and component parts, provided beginning on the opposite page, the usefulness of the "sentence sub-concept" as compared to the "single-word sub-concept" is clearly evident.

The following poem supports the need, in curriculum development, to cast concepts and sub-concepts in the form of sentences. It also illustrates the way in which the varying experiences of individuals affect concept formation.

"The Blind Men and the Elephant"*

by John Godfrey Saxe

It was six men of Indostan
    To learning much inclined,
Who went to see the elephant
    (Though all of them were blind),
That each by observation
    Might satisfy his mind.

The First approached the elephant,
    And, happening to fall
Against his broad and sturdy side,
    At once began to bawl:
"God bless me! but the elephant
    Is nothing but a wall!"

The Second, feeling of the tusk,
    Cried: "Ho! what have we here
So very round and smooth and sharp?
    To me 'tis mighty clear
This wonder of an elephant
    Is very like a spear!"

The Third approached the animal,
    And, happening to take
The squirming trunk within his hands,
    Thus boldly up and spake:
"I see," quoth he, "the elephant
    Is very like a snake!"

The Fourth reached out his eager hand,
    And felt about the knee:
"What most this wondrous beast is like
    Is mighty plain," quoth he;
"'Tis clear enough the elephant
    Is very like a tree."

The Fifth, who chanced to touch the ear,
    Said: "E'en the blindest man
Can tell what this resembles most;
    Deny the fact who can,
This marvel of an elephant
    Is very like a fan!"

The Sixth no sooner had begun
    About the beast to grope,
Than, seizing on the swinging tail
    That fell within his scope,
"I see," quoth he, "the elephant
    Is very like a rope!"

And so these men of Indostan
    Disputed loud and long,
Each in his own opinion
    Exceeding stiff and strong,
Though each was partly in the right,
    And all were in the wrong!

*So, oft in theologic wars
    The disputants, I ween,
Rail on in utter ignorance
    Of what each other mean,
And prate about an elephant
    Not one of them has seen!*

*David L. George (ed.), *The Family of Best Loved Poems* (New York: Doubleday and Company, Inc., 1952).

(Continued on page 58)

ILP 2—Lesson 2   57

Let us now look at concepts at varying levels of abstraction in order to relate these levels to the levels shown in Figure 1.

Level 1 (topic for a course of study): Agriculture is one of America's basic industries.

> *Level 2* (topic for a unit): The dominant theme in American history, until the present century, was Western agricultural expansion.
>
> > *Level 3* (major concept for an ILP): The Homestead Act made grants of 160-acre plots to people who would settle on and develop such plots.
> >
> > > *Level 4* (sub-concept for an ILP lesson): Homesteading land helped settle the West.
> > >
> > > *Level 4* (sub-concept for an ILP lesson): A homestead had to be developed for several years before title to the property could be secured.
> > >
> > > etc.

C. Read:

Sample Major Concept, Skill, and Value Statements with Component Parts

Listed below are three examples of major topics (one each in the concept, skill, and value categories) together with suggested component parts. An ILP could be effectively constructed around each of these examples.

(1) *Major Concept* (primary level, science): Magnets are metallic devices which exert a force that is an important source of power.

   Component Parts
   (a) Magnets can push and pull certain materials.
   (b) Magnets can push and pull each other.
   (c) Magnets are made from iron and steel.
   (d) Magnets attract through many materials.
   etc.

(2) *Major Skill* (intermediate level, physical education): Demonstrate correct, rudimentary form for executing the reel from the "Virginia Reel."

   Component Parts
   (a) The head couple bow and swing each other by locking right elbows. This action is executed in the center and at the head of the reel

(Continued from page 56)

The student, when forced to use a one-word concept, skill, or value as a guide to learning, is like a blind man approaching an elephant—he lacks sufficient information to accurately perceive his objectives. For this reason, the writer of the ILP must invest the selected concept, skill, or value with precise meaning according to the needs and levels of the intended learner. Obviously, to one with no previous experience with elephants, an elephant can be almost anything. Hence, to avoid mis-learning, the concept of "elephantness" would need to be placed within a statement which would define the structural or functional properties of the concept, as follows:

(1) An elephant is a large, gray animal with a trunk, tusks, and big ears.

(2) An elephant is a pachyderm.

(3) An elephant is a vertebrate mammal which . . .

(4) An elephant is . . .

formation. The head couple return to their initial positions.

(b) The head gent crosses to the opposite side of the reel formation and swings the second lady while the head lady crosses similarly and swings the second gent. Both actions are executed by the respective couples locking left elbows.

(c) The head couple return to the center of the reel formation and again swing each other by locking right elbows.

(d) The head couple repeat the actions described in parts (b) and (c) above with the third and subsequent couples until all couples in the reel formation have completed the swing.

(3) *Major Value* (secondary level, music): Listening to music is an enjoyable experience.

Component Parts

(a) Enjoyment of music is dependent upon a combination of factors including the listener's degree of musical understanding or sophistication, extra-musical associations, physiological responses, and familiarity with the particular selection being listened to.

(b) One of the most appealing and pervasive aspects of music is its function as a powerful form of communication at both general levels (e.g., moods and emotions) and more specific levels (e.g., ideas and experiences).

(c) A person may have many "favorite" kinds or pieces of music depending on his prevailing mood, his activities, and his emotional needs at the time of the listening experience.

(d) Enjoyment of and response to different types of music is often a highly individualized "happening" because of the considerable degree of ego involvement which characterizes the listening experience.

etc.

D. Do:

Additional Concept Development and Analysis

Select one or more of the following items according to your interests or teaching field. Use the selected item (or items) as the focus for writing one or more major concept, skill, or value statements together with statements of the component parts of each. Be sure that each statement you develop contains a complete and meaningful idea.

(1) Prime numbers are . . .
(2) Good grooming requires . . .
(3) A symphony is . . .
(4) Basketball players should . . .
(5) Making beef stock . . .

(6) Gravity . . .
(7) Student strikes and sit-ins . . .

The items above are only a few suggestions to get you started in the area of developing major and component concept, skill, and value statements. You should practice writing such statements in your subject area and at your teaching level.

CHECK YOUR PROGRESS

In the self-test for Lesson 1 in this ILP, you were asked to write major concept, skill, and value statements around which you could build ILPs appropriate to your teaching level and field. You are now being asked to construct statements for the component parts of those ideas. Of course, you may wish to begin by examining and revising your original major ideas somewhat based on your study of Lesson 2. Once you have settled on acceptable major concept, skill, and value statements, proceed to develop statements of component parts.

SELF-TEST KEY

If the statements of the major concepts, skills, and values and their component parts are appropriate for an ILP to be used at your teaching level and field, you are well on your way toward building an ILP. You may find the following questions helpful in evaluating your work thus far:

(1) Is each of the component parts you have identified a logical and relevant segment of the major concept, skill, or value?

(2) Has the number of component parts become so large and cumbersome that it would be best to create two or more ILPs rather than retaining all of the material in only one?

(3) If the major topic and component parts are skills (rather than concepts or values), is each discrete operation enumerated?

A further check on the quality of your work could be obtained by asking one or more students at the level for which the statements were designed to read the material for comprehension and, subsequently, to use it as a brief guide to learning. This type of field test will provide you with another indication as to whether or not you have met the learning objective for Lesson 2.

If you have completed the self-test for Lesson 2 and are satisfied with the results of your efforts in constructing major and component concept, skill, and value statements, turn to the next page and take the post-test for ILP 2.

On the other hand, if you experienced difficulty with the self-tests in either Lessons 1 or 2 in this ILP, you may wish to (1) review the basic points covered in ILP 2, (2)

POST-TEST FOR ILP 2

(1) Identify each item in the list of concepts, skills, and values below by placing C, S, or V in the spaces provided (100 percent accuracy is required).

........(a) Numbers have magnitude and direction.
........(b) Obtain uniform micrometer readings by holding the micrometer properly, i.e., with the little finger around the frame.
........(c) The Maori Poi-Poi is an action dance requiring a high degree of skill development.
........(d) The passé composé, a French tense which indicates an action completed in the past, is composed of a form of *avoir* and the past participle of another verb.
........(e) Paint one example each of the following color schemes: monochromatic, analogous, and complementary.
........(f) The habit of smoking has negative physiological effects on growing boys and girls.
........(g) A "round character" in literature is a character which has a number of complex traits that give dimension to his personality.
........(h) It is important that each individual be recognized as unique.
........(i) Demonstrate correct form while executing the standing broad jump.
........(j) All human beings need exposure to music as one of mankind's primary art forms.

(2) In a subject area and at a learning level of your choice, write simple, complete statements for a major idea and its component parts in each of the following categories: (a) concept, (b) skill, and (c) value.

discuss the apparent problem areas with one or more of your peers, or (3) schedule an individual conference with your instructor (where possible). Then, when you feel ready, take the post-test for ILP 2.

Use the post-test key (following page) for checking your responses on the post-test. When you are satisfied with your achievement of the objectives for ILP 2 as determined by the post-test results, you may choose either to proceed with quest activities in this ILP or, instead, to go directly to another ILP. If you choose quest, several suggestions are provided below. If you desire a more structured course of action at this point, you may wish to go to ILP 3 in which the techniques and values of writing and using learning objectives in ILPs are considered.

QUEST

You may wish to explore further in the area of the structuring of knowledge according to concepts, skills, and values. If so, some possible suggestions are provided below. As is our usual pattern with quest, however, you are not limited to these suggestions; you may choose to explore any related area of your interest.

A. What procedure would you use in developing a complete set (at a specified learning level) of the major concepts, skills, or values needed to teach a unit or course for which you are currently responsible?

B. Around what topics in your teaching field could you identify clusters of concepts (or skills or values) and their component parts which could be readily developed into several series of related ILPs? How could such ILPs be most effectively used in your current teaching situation?

C. Could you devise an action research project appropriate to your teaching situation which would support and further develop your understanding of the psychological basis for concept and value formation?

D. Can you identify a major idea at a specified learning level in your teaching field which would require component parts representing all three domains—the cognitive, affective, and psychomotor?

POST-TEST KEY FOR ILP 2

(1) (a) C   (c) C   (e) S   (g) C   (i) S
     (b) S   (d) C   (f) C   (h) V   (j) V

(2) To evaluate your response to item 2, use the keys to (a) the pre-test for this ILP, and (b) the self-tests for Lessons 1 and 2 of this ILP.

ILP 3

WHAT CHANGES WILL OCCUR?

Learning Objectives

CONCEPT

The development and use of ILPs are dependent on a description of the behaviors which result when the learner acquires concepts, skills, and values.

SUB-CONCEPTS

Objectives written to assist in developing and using ILPs are statements describing the expected, observable behaviors of a student when he has learned a given concept, skill, or value. Such statements are called learning objectives.

Learning objectives serve three primary purposes: (1) instructional planning, (2) motivation, and (3) evaluation.

When a teacher gives a student the objectives for the student's learning, the teacher is taking the first step toward individualized, continuous progress, self-paced learning.

LEARNING OBJECTIVES

Given a written list of objectives, you should be able to identify those examples which are stated behaviorally and those which are not. (A "behavioral" objective is defined as one which includes three essential parts: an action, a context, and a criterion of performance.) In addition, you should be able to identify, or supply if missing or improperly written, each of the three essential parts of each objective on the list.

Based on a component concept, skill, or value statement of your own choosing, you should be able to write at least one learning objective which contains all three essential parts.

PRE-TEST FOR ILP 3

(1) Identify as "behavioral" or "non-behavioral" each of the objectives in the following list (where a "behavioral" objective is defined as one which includes three essential parts—an action, a context, and a criterion of performance):

(a) When you are evaluated, you will be given copies of the following four poems: "The Raven" by Edgar Allan Poe, "Sea Fever" by John Masefield, "Fog" by Carl Sandburg, and "My Shadow" by Robert Louis Stevenson. In addition, you will be given copies of eight other poems (unfamiliar to you) written by the same four poets. You should be able to correctly name the poet for at least six of the eight additional poems.

(b) You should be able to discover the mechanical advantage of the pulley.

(c) Your teacher will organize a small group composed of not more than ten students. You should be able to describe at least one way that the U.S. system of federal government could be improved. Your suggestion should be different from ways suggested by the other nine members of your small group.

(d) You should be able to identify the copyright date, publisher, and call number.

(e) You should be able to perceive how to solve quadratic equations using the quadratic formula.

(2) For each of the above objectives which you labeled as "behavioral," identify each of the three essential parts. For those which you labeled as "non-behavioral," identify or supply each of the parts.

(3) If you are writing an ILP as you read this book, you may already have written statements of major concepts, skills, and values as well as statements of their component parts. In any case, select a component concept, skill, or value and write one or more learning objectives based on the statement you selected.

(4) Describe at least one way each in which learning objectives help to accomplish the following teaching-learning tasks: (a) instructional planning, (b) motivation, and (c) evaluation.

You should be able to describe at least one way each in which learning objectives help to accomplish the following teaching-learning tasks: (1) instructional planning, (2) motivation, and (3) evaluation.

Take the pre-test for ILP 3 (opposite page). When you have completed the pre-test, turn to the key beginning on the next page.

If you are satisfied with your pre-test results on questions 1, 2, and 3, you may wish to skip Lesson 1 in this ILP. Question 4 is designed to evaluate whether or not you need to study Lesson 2. If you are using this book on an individual basis, you will have to make your own decision as to which lessons or ILP you could most profitably consider next. If you are working with an instructor, he may wish to help you evaluate your pre-test results and prescribe specific or alternative learning activities from Lessons 1 and 2 or another ILP.

POST-TEST KEY FOR ILP 3

(1)   (a) behavioral   (c) behavioral   (e) non-behavioral
         (b) non-behavioral   (d) non-behavioral

(2) The three essential parts of each objective can be identified or supplied as follows. (Of course, in any objective where material must be supplied, you may have written equally valid learning objectives which differ considerably in terms of content from the material given below. However, your ingredients should be of a type which is comparable.)

     (a) This statement is a properly written learning objective. The objective also has elements of inquiry built into it.

         Action: *name* the poets
         Context: given copies of the four poems, "The Raven" by Edgar Allan Poe, "Sea Fever" by John Masefield, "Fog" by Carl Sandburg, and "My Shadow" by Robert Louis Stevenson, and eight other poems (unfamiliar to you) written by the same four poets
         Criterion: at least six correct out of eight

     (b) Based on the objective as written, the reader is not given definitive information regarding the desired behavior, its context, or the level of performance required. Hence, none of the three parts of a learning objective are present. If the teacher simply wants the student to discover that certain arrangements of pulleys can result in decreased effort, then the learning objective could contain the following essential parts:

         Actions: *construct* a pulley system and *compare (measure)* the amount of effort needed with and without pulleys
         Context: given pulleys, string, and an object to lift
         Criteria: at least three different pulley arrangements should be constructed

     (c) The action, context, and criterion of this objective are adequate if one assumes that the student realizes that he should have several (perhaps as many as ten) improvements in mind so that he is sure to have at least one that is different from those suggested by the other members of the small group.

         Action: *describe* one way in which the U.S. system of federal government could be improved
         Context: a small group composed of not more than ten students with the teacher present
         Criterion: originality with reference to improvements suggested by the student's peers

(Pre-Test Key continued on page 70)

LESSON 1

SUB-CONCEPT

Objectives written to assist in developing and using ILPs are statements describing the expected, observable behaviors of a student when he has learned a given concept, skill, or value. Such statements are called learning objectives.

LEARNING OBJECTIVES

Given a written list of objectives, you should be able to identify those examples which are stated behaviorally and those which are not. (A "behavioral" objective is defined as one which includes three essential parts: an action, a context, and a criterion of performance.) In addition, you should be able to identify, or supply if missing or improperly written, each of the three essential parts of each objective on the list.

Based on a component concept, skill, or value statement of your own choosing, you should be able to write at least one learning objective which contains all three essential parts.

Proceed directly to the first learning activity and read the "Introduction to Learning Objectives" which we have provided. Then, read the second learning activity, which is designed to help you make decisions concerning alternative ways of meeting your own learning needs.

LEARNING ACTIVITIES

A. Read:

Introduction to Learning Objectives

At the beginning of this lesson you were provided with two learning objectives. These particular learning objectives could also have been stated in the following more general terms: *To gain an understanding of the type of learning objective in which observable behaviors are described.*

PRE-TEST KEY FOR ILP 3 (continued from page 68)

    (d)   The desired action or behavior on the part of the student is specified in this objective. The context, on the other hand, is completely missing in the objective as originally stated (one of several possible contexts is provided below). The criterion is implied to be 100% (mastery), which is acceptable if the student who receives a mastery objective (1) can reasonably be expected to achieve such mastery, and (2) is permitted to re-study the material and correct any initial errors which he might make.

    Action: *identify* the copyright date, publisher, and call number
    Context: given access to a library card catalog and given the titles or authors of five books in that particular collection
    Criterion: for all five books with 100% accuracy

    (e)   Because "perception" is a mental process, it is not directly observable. Thus, the action word needs revision. In addition, the context and the criterion of performance are only partially supplied. Mathematics teachers will note at least one potential problem in writing a learning objective dealing with the use of the quadratic formula in solving quadratic equations. Many quadratic equations are readily solved, depending on the insight of the student, by factoring or completing the square instead of applying the quadratic formula. For this reason, we have revised the learning objective so that the student must show his work.

    Action: *demonstrate* how to solve quadratic equations and show your work
    Context: given three quadratic equations in the form $ax^2 + bx + c = 0$
    Criteria: the process which you use must employ the quadratic formula and must be correct in all three cases

(3)   Ask your instructor to help you evaluate the statement of the concept, skill, or value and the corresponding learning objective(s) which you wrote. If you are using this book without assistance from a teacher, seek help from a colleague who is experienced in writing such learning objectives. Whether or not there is anyone to assist you with an evaluation of your work on this item, you may find the following questions useful as evaluative guides.

(Pre-Test Key continued on page 72)

Does the format of the general objective just stated look familiar to you? All of us surely have written or seen objectives that started with the preposition "to" and that contained words like "understand," "know," "appreciate," or "enjoy." There really is nothing wrong with such general objectives. In fact, a useful technique in warming up to writing specific learning objectives is to start by writing general objectives. You can even go a step further by writing a "rationale" for the student in which you explain why he should incorporate a particular teacher-made general objective into his own set of personal objectives. Unfortunately, however, educators often stop writing objectives at this point. They do not go on to restate the general objectives in more specific terms. That is, they neglect to tell the student what he is going to have to do at evaluation time to show the teacher that he has learned or acquired a desired concept, skill, or value. As a result, many teachers have been "turned off" on objectives because there has been no payoff in the classroom.

Statements which (1) tell the student where he is going, (2) guide him in deciding how he will get there, and (3) allow him to gauge when he has arrived are given several different names by educators. You will see them referred to as "instructional objectives," "behavioral objectives," "performance objectives," and possibly other names. Each term means approximately the same thing and, thus, the particular term used is more often representative of author preference than of basic differences in meaning among the terms. For example, we feel that the word "instructional" places too much emphasis on what the teacher does, and that the word "behavioral" occasionally is misunderstood because of its good-bad connotations. The word "performance" is a good one to use; it places emphasis on observability. However, because we are interested in students being given these objectives to help them guide their own learning, we call them *learning objectives.*

You have seen many examples of learning objectives in this book. Most of them contain three basic parts: (1) an action—what the student is supposed to be able to do when he is evaluated—which is communicated by means of action words such as "identify," "name," "describe," "construct," "order," and "demonstrate"; (2) a context—the conditions under which the student will be evaluated—which might be implied or stated in a phrase frequently beginning with the word "given"; and (3) a criterion—the level of performance expected of the student—in which quality and/or quantity expectations are stated. ("Action terms" in learning objectives are discussed in greater detail in the next lesson. Numerous examples of the most useful kinds of action words are provided.)

B. Do:

Making a Decision

This is a good place to insert some questions which might help you make your own decisions. We will offer suggestions for your selection of learning activities which

PRE-TEST KEY FOR ILP 3 (continued from page 70)

  (a) Does the learning objective ask for a behavior which clearly relates to the component concept, skill, or value statement?

  (b) Are the conditions under which the student will be evaluated completely clear?

  (c) Is the performance which is called for an observable or measurable one?

  (d) Is the student's level of performance (or degree of attainment of the criteria) stated implicitly or explicitly? Which is preferable?

(4) Learning objectives help in the following ways:

  (a) *Instructional planning.*—The teacher's task in providing students with learning materials and activities is directly related to learning objectives. The teacher can provide materials and activities which require either identical behaviors or analogous behaviors as compared to those described in the learning objectives. When the student is given the objectives for his learning, he can select or find learning materials and activities to help him achieve those objectives. In cases where sequence is optional, he can even plan the order in which he will achieve the objectives. Thus, objectives enable the student to modify his behavior from that of following directions for each learning step to that of reasoned decision making regarding the manner and sequence in which he will achieve learning objectives.

  (b) *Motivation.*—Learning objectives provide the teacher with the targets toward which he will attempt to stimulate action on the part of students. Without learning objectives, such stimulation might be inappropriately focused, thus resulting in misdirected and ineffective action or no action at all. The teacher's purpose in motivating the student is to help the student make the teacher-designed learning objectives the student's own. If the student can see purpose and relevance in what the teacher would like him to do, he probably will be willing to become responsibly involved. Conditions which interest the student in initiating learning objectives of his own also should be provided.

  (c) *Evaluation.*—The preparation of assessment methods should be based directly on learning objectives. Learning objectives quickly lose the advantages described above, both for the teacher and for the learner, if the form and content of student evaluation differs from that which was established in the objectives. Properly written learning objectives permit sufficient flexibility for alternative evaluation modes (when alternatives are desirable) while still adhering to the intent of the objectives. In addition, the student's ability to self-evaluate is developed more readily when he can focus on learning instead of guessing at the teacher's objectives.

ILP 3—Lesson 1

you may elect to follow or not, depending on your interest and skill with regard to preparing learning objectives.

1. Do you feel that general objectives are adequate for meeting the needs of you and your students, and that writing more specific learning objectives is a waste of time?

    No— Go on to Question 2!

    Yes— a. You may wish to read the poem on page vii of Robert Mager's book titled, *Developing Attitude Toward Learning.*
    b. Or, read pages 1 and 2 of Mager's book titled, *Preparing Instructional Objectives.*
    c. Or, if you teach such subjects as science, home economics, business machines, or industrial arts, read the unnumbered page between pages 2 and 3 of *Preparing Instructional Objectives.*
    d. Or, if you teach such subjects as social studies, art, music, or literature, read the poem on page 69 of *Developing Attitude Toward Learning.*
    e. Or, go on to Learning Activity C. You may change your mind later and see some value to our sequence.

2. Are you concerned about writing learning objectives that get at what is "really important" in your course rather than just knowledge-recall and rote memorization types of learning?

    Yes— Good! You should have this concern. Skip the next question and go to Learning Activity C. Also, you will find that some of the concerns which you have in this area are dealt with in Lesson 2 of this ILP.

    No— There are at least two good reasons for a negative response to this question. First, you may realize that higher levels of learning such as analysis and synthesis have as their bases less complicated and less abstract levels such as knowledge and comprehension. This is a valid point, but at the same time you should be *concerned* about the higher levels of learning, although not necessarily at this stage in your preparation of learning objectives.

    Second, you may have decided to write an ILP as you read this book. As a result you may want to quickly get to those learning activities which, when completed, provide you with further ingredients for your ILP. Go ahead—but first read the

You probably noticed in Learning Activity B that the student is encouraged to control his own learning experiences. In the past, educators have called this type of student control and participation "teacher-pupil planning." Such involvement is even more important in continuous progress materials than in group-paced instructional methods.

Motivational theory has long supported the need for meaningful participation by the student in his own learning experiences. See the following:

(1) Fletcher G. Watson, *What Psychology Can We Trust?* (New York: Bureau of Publications, Teachers College, Columbia University, 1961), 19 pp.

(2) Asahel D. Woodruff, *Basic Concepts of Teaching* (San Francisco: Chandler Publishing Company, 1961), 238 pp. See especially Chapter 12: "Motivation," pp. 207-215.

In addition, research indicates that learning efficiency is improved when the student is given considerable control over his own learning. See the following:

(1) Robert F. Mager, "Learner-Controlled Instruction, 1958-1964," *Programmed Instruction,* IV (November, 1964), 1, 8, 10-11.

(2) _____, "The Need to State Our Educational Intents," *Technology and Innovation in Education* (New York: Frederick A. Praeger, Publishers, 1968), pp. 35-40.

third question below and then proceed to the self-test for this lesson. You can return to the remainder of the materials in this lesson at a later time if you find that you need greater depth or understanding in a particular area.

3. Are you ready to write the learning objective for an ILP appropriate to your teaching level and field?

No— Go on to Learning Activity C.

Yes— Apparently you feel that you are ready to demonstrate your achievement of the second learning objective for this lesson. Turn to the self-test for this lesson.

C. Select:

Books

1. Robert F. Mager, *Preparing Instructional Objectives* (Palo Alto, California: Fearon Publishers, 1962), 60 pp.

   This short book has become a must for those who are interested in writing learning objectives. Read it, but do not end your education on learning objectives with this book because it provides examples primarily of lower level content or subject matter objectives.

2. Robert F. Mager, *Developing Attitude Toward Learning* (Palo Alto, California: Fearon Publishers, 1968), 104 pp.

   Mager's book is a source of encouragement to teachers who would like to obtain some student feedback as a guide to developing positive attitudes toward learning in the particular subject matter area in which they teach. The book is somewhat more difficult reading than *Preparing Instructional Objectives,* but is well worth the effort.

3. Miriam B. Kapfer, *Behavioral Objectives in Curriculum Development: Selected Readings and Bibliography* (Englewood Cliffs, New Jersey: Educational Technology Publications, Inc., 1971).

   This volume is a major compilation of outstanding papers dealing with the specification of objectives for education. It is organized in a functionally useful manner for the classroom teacher and curriculum writer. Part I of the book, "Behavioral Objectives—An Overview of What, Why, and How," is especially appropriate for your reading at this time.

4. Paul Plowman, "Unit 1: Behavioral Objectives and Teacher Success," *Behavioral Objectives Extension Service* (Chicago, Illinois: Science Research Associates, Inc., 1968-69).

Plowman prepared a series of eight units published monthly during the 1968-69 school year by SRA. The units deal with behavioral objectives for grades K through 12. Unit One (32 pp.) provides a good overview of the subject of behavioral objectives, while Units Two through Eight deal with behavioral objectives in specific subject matter areas.

Filmstrip

W. James Popham and Eva L. Baker, *Educational Objectives.* 25 min., 37 frames, color. Vimcet Associates, Los Angeles, California, 1967.

This filmstrip is the first in a series of seven illustrated filmstrips with accompanying audio-taped narrations which are available from Vimcet Associates. The filmstrip illustrations are entertaining; however, considerable pause-time is provided on the audio-tape, making active participation a must. If possible, compare your responses with the instructor's manual after viewing the entire filmstrip.

CHECK YOUR PROGRESS

You have already had the opportunity in the pre-test for this ILP of identifying or supplying the three essential parts of several learning objectives. How well did you do? It might be profitable for you to return to items 1 and 2 on the pre-test and key in order to review the five objectives provided there and re-test yourself.

Of course, the most important learning outcome of this lesson is that you should be able to write learning objectives. If you have not done so already, you should try your hand at it now. If you have studied ILP 2 prior to this ILP, you will already have written major and component concept, skill, and value statements. It helps, when you are attempting to write learning objectives, if you already have decided on *what* you want the students to learn. Then you can decide on the behaviors which might result from that learning. The specification of these behaviors is the meat of learning objectives.

SELF-TEST KEY

You know, by this time, what a learning objective is. The problem now is in being sure that you have communicated adequately the educational intent of the objectives which you wrote. Ask one of your colleagues to read your learning objectives, or, better yet, ask one of your students to read them. If someone else can read your objectives and then give you examples of ways in which evaluation might occur (which are similar to evaluation methods you would devise), you probably

Quest can be placed at the end of each lesson in an ILP (as found on the opposite page) or it may be reserved for placement after the ILP post-test (as has been our practice in the two previous ILPs in this book). Of course, questions which are designed to stimulate inquiry while *focusing on* the learning objectives in a lesson belong in the learning activities section of that lesson. By contrast, the questions which are placed in Quest should *go beyond* the learning objectives in the lesson or ILP for which the quest section is being designed.

ILP 3—Lesson 1

have done your job well. Just be sure that you have included all three of the essential parts of a learning objective in each example, or be able to justify why you have not.

If you are satisfied with your achievement of the objectives for this lesson, move ahead to Lesson 2 or to another ILP. If the results of the self-test indicate that you need greater depth, you may wish to review or use more extensively some of the sources suggested under "Learning Activities" in this lesson. Also, you may wish to engage in quest prior to continuing in this or another ILP.

QUEST

The questions provided below are designed to take you beyond the objectives for this lesson.

A. What is the significance for concept formation of the word "internalization" as used by the writers of the *Taxonomy of Educational Objectives?*

B. How can learning objectives be written which will promote inquiry in your curricular content area? which will promote creativity? community involvement?

C. How can you provide for student feedback so that you have a sound basis on which to revise your learning objectives?

D. Have you any further questions regarding learning objectives that are particularly relevant to your needs? If so, discuss the questions with your teacher (if available) or with a colleague. Then pursue the questions to whatever breadth or depth you desire.

LESSON 2

SUB-CONCEPTS

Learning objectives serve three primary purposes: (1) instructional planning, (2) motivation, and (3) evaluation.

When a teacher gives a student the objectives for the student's learning, the teacher is taking the first step toward individualized, continuous progress, self-paced learning.

LEARNING OBJECTIVE

You should be able to describe at least one way each in which learning objectives help to accomplish the following teaching-learning tasks: (1) instructional planning, (2) motivation, and (3) evaluation.

The learning activities in this lesson are designed to increase your understanding of the purposes and nature of learning objectives. You may find it useful to refer frequently to the learning objectives you wrote while completing the last lesson and, if necessary, alter them according to new insights which you gain. Based on the level of skill development which you demonstrated in the preceding lesson, choose from among the learning activities which follow.

LEARNING ACTIVITIES

A. Read:

The Role of Learning Objectives in Instructional Planning

In order to discuss the role of objectives in instructional planning, we need to introduce what may be new vocabulary to some readers (particularly to those who chose to do this ILP prior to ILP 2). As a result of attempts to classify or create a "taxonomy" of educational objectives, three principal categories or "domains" have been identified: (1) the "cognitive," involving the thought processes; (2) the "affective," relating primarily to the emotions; and (3) the "psychomotor," involving principally the mental-muscular processes. These three domains have been further divided into levels or hierarchies which, although not behavioral *per se,* are useful as tools in writing learning objectives. A fourth category also has been suggested by Nolan C. Kearney (1953), M. Ray Loree (1965), Elizabeth Simpson (1967), and perhaps others. This category has been called the "action pattern" domain, and it describes the behavior of the student as he uses the knowledge, understanding, and skills that he has learned. These action pattern behaviors also are

Occasionally authors, reports, or articles will be referred to on right-hand pages. These normally will be given without footnotes, but the reader will be able to find complete citations to these materials included among the learning activities of the particular lesson or ILP.

*

APPROACHES TO HANDLING AFFECTIVE DOMAIN OBJECTIVES

Two approaches appear to lend themselves to the development of affective domain learning objectives. The first approach begins with a statement of a broad or long-range general objective followed by a series of specific learning objectives developed as behavioral sub-statements which stem from a positive attitude toward the general objective. For example, Arthur M. Cohen (1969) provided an illustration of this approach in the three related sentences which follow:

Broad or long-range general objective:

The student will exercise the privileges and responsibilities of democratic citizenship.

Resultant behavioral sub-statements:

The student, if eligible, will voluntarily register to vote within six months following the course.

Prior to the next general election, the student will voluntarily campaign for a candidate by working in his office or distributing handbills for a period of not less than forty hours.

You will note that each of the specific behavioral sub-statements above contains all three components of a properly written learning objective:

Actions: register to vote; campaign for a candidate by working in his office or distributing handbills
Context: voluntarily
Criteria: either he registers or he does not within six months; for a period of not less than forty hours

We have called this approach to amplifying (or operationalizing) a general goal the "accumulation of behaviors" approach. For example, behaviors such as the following might be used to further extend the series of statements which behavioralize the general objective above:

Prior to the next election, the student will voluntarily contribute at least $10.00 to the campaign fund of a candidate of his choice.

(Continued on page 84)

an expression of the student's attitudes and interests because they are the behaviors he normally displays in the various "real world" or "in-life" situations he faces.

There are problems, however, in using the taxonomy approach. Affective learning is most often a *part of* cognitive and psychomotor learning rather than a separate entity. It cannot be as readily isolated for teaching-learning purposes as for taxonomical purposes. Usually, growth in affective behaviors is based on or is the product of cognitive and skill learning and can be best assessed on a long-range basis (which often is not useful as a means of determining affective growth in courses extending only for a semester or a year). In other words, affective learning usually supports and results from cognitive and psychomotor learning but is more difficult to measure on a short-term basis. On occasion, we teach *directly* for affective learning (and thus develop ILPs for this purpose) because we wish to help students *conceptualize* given values rather than simply "acquire" them.

In the following paragraphs, the emphasis is on the conceptualization process in the use of ILPs. Approaches that promote definition of affective goals to be acquired on a long-range basis are included in the Teacher's Supplement beginning on the opposite page.

The levels of objectives in educational planning.—At least three levels of educational objectives and planning can be identified as meaningful for the classroom teacher. The first and most abstract level is represented by statements of educational principles and general objectives such as those which frequently are adopted by school boards and other policy making bodies.

The second level is best represented by district-level curriculum guides in which a relatively small number of summative-type behavioral objectives represent the learning outcomes of a corresponding number of *major* concepts, skills, and values in an area or course of study. The current trend in developing curriculum guides is to state such cumulative kinds of objectives behaviorally, although many curriculum guides still contain non-behavioral objectives at this level of planning.

Daily planning, whether for the teacher in a lesson plan book or for the student in an ILP, necessitates a third, more finite level of learning objectives. Such objectives are written to describe behaviors which result from attainment of *component* (as compared to major) concepts, skills, and values.

Each of these three levels of objectives is important because each guides the development of the next more specific level. However, because you as a teacher or building administrator are involved daily in implementing district-level curriculum guides, it is especially important that you learn to analyze objectives from the middle level to the third or most specific level.

(Continued from page 82)

> Prior to the next election, the student will voluntarily assist with the local campaign of voter registration for a period of not less than forty hours.
>
> On the next election day, the student will voluntarily assist voters in getting to their polling places by serving as (for example) an unpaid baby sitter or driver for a period of not less than four hours.
>
> During the six-month period following the course, the student will voluntarily attend at least one public meeting per month of local governmental bodies such as the county commissioners, city council, township trustees, or school board.

A sample "accumulation of behaviors" in the arts might begin with the general objective, "The student will develop appreciation for various forms of artistic expression." Sample statements which amplify and behavioralize this general objective might include the following:

> Within the year following enrollment in a course in The Arts in American Life, the student will voluntarily attend at least five art exhibits, concerts, and/or plays.
>
> Within the year following enrollment in the course, the student will voluntarily purchase not fewer than five recordings of classical music.
>
> Within the year following enrollment in the course, the student will voluntarily devote an average of one evening a month to fund-raising activities for the local symphony society.
>
> Within the year following enrollment in the course, the student will voluntarily and independently study the interpretation of music through the media of dancing or painting by (for example) checking out appropriate references from the library, joining a local modern dance club, or choosing a particular piece of music to interpret by means of water colors or oils.

Other examples of the "accumulation of behaviors" approach can be found in the Albert F. Eiss and Mary Blatt Harbeck publication, *Behavioral Objectives in the Affective Domain* (1969). In this monograph, an attempt is made to operationalize some of the affective behaviors of the "scientifically literate" citizen.

In each example provided above of the "accumulation of behaviors" approach, evaluation of a learner's achievement of the broad or long-range general objective would be determined primarily on the basis of the *number* of specific sub-behaviors that he evidenced rather than by the appearance or intensity of any one particular behavior.

(Continued on page 86)

Action-describing words in educational planning.—The elementary school science program, *Science—A Process Approach,* sponsored by the American Association for the Advancement of Science, produced a continuum of nine performance or action-describing terms. The items in the continuum, although somewhat overlapping, begin with simple behaviors and extend to more complex or higher level behaviors: (1) "identify," (2) "name," (3) "order," (4) "describe," (5) "distinguish," (6) "construct," (7) "demonstrate," (8) "state a rule," and (9) "apply a rule."

Howard J. Sullivan (undated monograph) distilled the nine AAAS action terms into six words which are more useful in writing behaviorally stated learning objectives. The six Sullivan terms in the continuum given below can be applied to all curricular areas. The continuum also includes equivalent terms and phrases for each of the six Sullivan behaviors and an explanation of the meaning of each basic behavior.

(1) IDENTIFY (equivalent terms and phrases—choose, compare, discriminate between or among, distinguish between or among, indicate, mark, match, select):

The learner indicates whether or not specified phenomena (objects, processes, or consequences) are members of a class when the name of the class is given.

(2) NAME (equivalent terms—designate, label, list, state):

The learner supplies the correct verbal label (orally or in writing) for one or more phenomena when the names are not given.

(3) DESCRIBE (equivalent terms and phrases—analyze, characterize, define, diagram, discuss, explain, replicate, report, represent, reproduce, tell how, tell what happens when):

The learner represents by words (a) the structure, qualities, and functions of objects, or (b) the consequences of processes and behaviors. In other words, the learner describes the critical properties of phenomena.

(4) CONSTRUCT (equivalent terms—build, draw, formulate, make, prepare, synthesize):

The learner puts together the parts making up a concept. Thus, he builds or produces a product such as a drawing, an article of clothing or furniture, a map, or an essay. The product itself is evaluated.

(Continued from page 84)

The second approach to developing learning objectives in the affective domain is simply a refinement of the first. It involves the amplification of non-behavioral general objectives with "*continua* of behaviors" rather than with "*accumulations* of behaviors." In other words, instead of stating a series of behaviors at unspecified levels, the behaviors are designed and listed so as to exhibit gradually increasing levels of sophistication. Consider the following general objective: "The student increasingly values human, book, and non-book learning resources." By focusing on the *degree of self-direction* involved in the process of selecting learning resources (as a manifestation of *valuing* learning resources), the following continuum of behaviors can be constructed:

1. When given an opportunity to choose study sources, including (a) activities with other people, (b) books, and (c) non-book materials, the student generally chooses his study sources from the same one of the three possible categories.

2. When given an opportunity to choose study sources, including (a) activities with other people, (b) books, and (c) non-book materials, the student generally chooses his study sources from two or three of the three possible categories.

3. When given an opportunity to choose study sources, including (a) activities with other people, (b) books, and (c) non-book materials, the student is able to discuss the reasons for his choices in terms of the quality and type of information anticipated in the sources he selected.

A similar continuum, in the affective area of "increasingly valuing the skills which are necessary for locating organized sources of information," is as follows:

1. When given a list of media citiations for an assigned topic or area of study, the student is able to locate from the list the media sources he will study.

2. When given index and card catalog entry words for an assigned topic or area of study, the student is able to use the entry words for locating the media sources he will study.

3. When given no citations or entry words for an assigned topic or area of study, (a) the student is able to determine possible entry words himself, and (b) by using indexes and the card catalog, he is able to use these entry words to locate the media sources he will study.

(Continued on page 88)

(5) ORDER (equivalent terms and phrases—arrange in a pattern, arrange in order, catalog, categorize, classify, list in order, outline, rank, relate, sequence):

The learner arranges two or more phenomena in a specified order. He may be given the names of the phenomena which he must order, he may be asked to name them himself as well as order them, or he may be asked to order them without having to provide verbal labels.

(6) DEMONSTRATE (equivalent terms and phrases—perform an experiment, perform the steps, role play, show the procedure, participate, show your work, simulate):

The learner performs a task according to pre-established or given specifications. The task may involve a number of behaviors including identifying, naming, describing, constructing, and ordering (or combinations of these). The procedures the learner follows in performing the task are of greater concern than the product which may result from those procedures.

Care must be taken in choosing the action word for a learning objective (1) so that verbal responses are not mistaken for concept formation, and (2) so that the action word maximizes observability while avoiding educational triteness. Selective use of the above list will help to avoid both of these pitfalls. In addition, the above terms can be used to introduce variety and increasingly sophisticated levels of performance into the lessons being prepared. Students who do not do well at such verbal behaviors as identifying, naming, and describing can still have successful experiences by selecting lessons (or objectives within lessons) which focus on the potentially non-verbal behaviors of constructing, ordering, and demonstrating. At the same time, terminal performances so frequently equated with paper-pencil testing can be replaced with a larger proportion of en route behavioral expectations.

B. Read:

The Role of Learning Objectives in Motivation

All of us, as teachers, hope that our students will develop positive attitudes toward the subject matter we teach. Certainly we hope that our students will not be more negative toward our favorite subject as a result of the contact we provide than they were before taking our course. Mager (1968) referred to such positive and negative attitudes as the "tendency to approach" or become involved in a given subject. The key ideas are these: (1) if we associate "positive conditions" with given subject matter, the student's tendency to approach that subject will increase; and (2) if we

(Continued from page 86)

A third example of the "continuum of behaviors" approach to affective objectives relates to the general goal, "The student increasingly values independent learning, as observed in his self-initiating and self-directing behaviors." This goal may be amplified by the following continuum of five behaviors:

1. Given a teacher-assigned delimited topic with assigned specified resources, the student follows directions.

2. Given a teacher-assigned delimited topic and assigned alternative resources, the student selects from alternative resources.

3. Given a teacher-assigned delimited topic, the student seeks his own resources.

4. Given a teacher-assigned broad topic, the student delimits the topic and seeks his own resources.

5. Given a student-initiated broad or delimited topic (in or out of school), the student delimits the topic as necessary and seeks his own resources.

It is important to note that all three sample continua are meaningful for affective growth, as well as for observation and measurement, *so long as* the student actually has available to him all of the "given" portions (in other words, the "condition" portions) of the enumerated behaviors. If the conditions are all consistently available, then the student can voluntarily choose the level at which he will operate, thus providing a measure of his affective development with respect to a given general objective in the affective domain.

Two additional points concerning the accumulation and continuum approaches to affective objectives should be mentioned. First, it may not be practical nor possible to behavioralize all affective objectives by means of the continuum approach. Instead, the accumulation approach should be used for those cases which cannot be refined as far as the continuum state. Second, even when the continuum approach is possible, it is not always entirely desirable that all learners operate only at a single step or end of the continuum; in other words, depending on the nature of each general objective which is behavioralized by means of the continuum approach, both the teacher and the learner should mutually agree on the specific sub-behaviors which are most important for indicating successful achievement of a particular affective general objective for each individual learner.

(Continued on page 90)

associate negative or "aversive conditions" with given subject matter, the student's tendency to approach that subject will decrease.

Once you have accomplished the task of writing learning objectives in a form which appeals to your students and in language which they can comprehend, an important problem in the area of motivation has been overcome. You now have something—the objective—toward which action can be stimulated. The most important motivating function of learning objectives is in their direct use by the student (1) to know what is expected of him, (2) to guide him in selecting his own learning activities, and (3) to help him evaluate his own progress in achieving the objectives.

However, there may be considerable difference, as any experienced teacher knows, between the teacher's objective and the student's objective. Even though the student may comprehend the teacher's statement of the objective for his learning, he may consider the objective to be unimportant because he is unable to relate it to a larger area of study. In addition, he may not know why the objective should have importance to him as an individual learner. Nevertheless, if he is a "good" student, he still may set about to achieve the objective. But such a student is depending on the teacher's authority, and if such dependency is consistently (if inadvertently) encouraged, the student will not develop the characteristics of an independent learner in that subject area. In other words, an aversive condition is being provided which may cause a decreased tendency on the part of the student to approach that subject both during and after taking the course.

On the other hand, the student will be motivated in a positive fashion if he is able to see that achievement of the objective will help him satisfy his own needs. This can be accomplished (1) by associating a behaviorally stated objective with its more general objective, and (2) by giving the student a rationale or reason for asking him to achieve the objective. These two strategies serve to identify the objective with its in-life referents. For example, consider the following statements from your own point of view as a learner whose in-life behaviors are those of teaching:

(1) *A non-behavioral general objective*: The learner is to develop an understanding of learning objectives.

(2) *A behavioral learning objective*: Given the statement of a concept in your own field, you should be able to write a learning objective and discuss its behaviorality. Each of the three components of a learning objective (the action, the context, and the criterion) must be included.

(3) *A rationale*: Learning objectives are important to you and to your students because they tell how your students are expected to demonstrate their achievement. In addition, learning objectives are the key elements in permitting your students to learn at their own best rates and in their own unique styles and sequences.

(Continued from page 88)

How do both of these approaches to the affective domain relate to curriculum development? The accumulation approach to writing behavioral objectives lends itself most readily to the evaluation of both the instructional program and individual student performance. The "continuum" approach to writing behavioral objectives is useful for evaluation also, but it is of greatest value in identifying and providing for continua of *conditions* (and therefore options) under which affective growth can occur.

*

Additional information on learning objectives may be found in the following sources:

Books

1. Aerospace Education Foundation, *Technology and Innovation in Education: Putting Educational Technology to Work in America's Schools* (New York: Frederick A. Praeger, Publishers, 1968), 149 pp.

2. Thorwald Esbensen, *Working with Individualized Instruction: The Duluth Experience* (Palo Alto, California: Fearon Publishers, 1968), 122 pp.

3. Robert F. Mager and Kenneth M. Beach, Jr., *Developing Vocational Instruction* (Palo Alto, California: Fearon Publishers, 1967), 83 pp. See especially Chapter 5: "Course Objectives," pp. 28-34.

Monograph

Asahel D. Woodruff and Janyce L. Taylor, *A Teaching Behavior Code* (Salt Lake City, Utah: The Utah State Board of Education, undated), 54 pp.

Although motivation may not result simply because the student knows what goal has been selected for him, the chances are very good that he will work toward the achievement of an objective if he sees a purpose or a reason for such effort. If he does, he will make the objective his own. This basic principle of motivation is just as important in ILPs as in other instructional approaches. Providing a rationale creates an additional positive (rather than aversive) condition that can be associated with the subject matter.

C. Read:

The Role of Learning Objectives in Evaluation

You may wish to review answer 4-c on the pre-test key for this ILP. The idea emphasized there, that *evaluation must accurately reflect the performance described in the student's learning objectives,* is basic to the success of an individualized learning system using ILPs. ILP 5 is devoted to evaluating student achievement in ILPs, and ILP 9 is concerned with evaluating the curriculum and supporting sub-systems. Therefore, our discussion here will be highly contracted in the interest of avoiding unnecessary duplication.

Looking briefly at evaluation from a broad perspective, objective-based measures, whether self-imposed or teacher-imposed, are valuable forms of feedback to the student, the teacher, and the curriculum designer. Such evaluation provides information about both the educational process (the school) and the educational product (the student). In other words, evaluation based on learning objectives demonstrates to the student the consequences of his behavior patterns—in this case, the results of his choices of learning activities and the extent of his study for achieving the learning objectives. It provides the teacher with insight as to the effectiveness and value of his teaching methods, curricular materials, and perhaps even his student learning objectives. And finally, it provides the curriculum designer with the focus necessary for mediating a lesson and with the basis for developing systems for regularly improving the learning materials.

D. Select:

Books

1. AAAS Commission on Science Education, *Response Sheets for the Guide for Inservice Instruction: Science—A Process Approach* (Washington, D.C.: American Association for the Advancement of Science, 1967), 80 pp.

2. Arthur M. Cohen, "Defining Instructional Objectives," *Systems Approach-*

es to Curriculum and Instruction in the Open-Door College, ed. B. Lamar Johnson (Los Angeles, California: University of California at Los Angeles, 1967), pp. 25-33.

3. Miriam B. Kapfer, *Behavioral Objectives in Curriculum Development: Selected Readings and Bibliography* (Englewood Cliffs, New Jersey: Educational Technology Publications, Inc., 1971). See especially Parts II through VIII dealing with the relationship of learning objectives to the teaching of values, individualized curricular systems, educational technology, evaluation, and various subject matter areas.

4. Nolan C. Kearney, *Elementary School Objectives* (New York: Russell Sage Foundation, 1953), 189 pp.

5. M. Ray Loree, "Relationship Among Three Domains of Educational Objectives," *Contemporary Issues in Home Economics: A Conference Report* (Washington, D.C.: National Education Association, 1965), pp. 69-80.

6. Robert F. Mager, *Developing Attitude Toward Learning* (Palo Alto, California: Fearon Publishers, 1968), 104 pp.

7. Elizabeth Simpson, "Educational Objectives—Four Domains," *Educational Media in Vocational and Technical Education: A Report of a National Seminar,* ed. Calvin J. Cotrell and Edward F. Hauck (Columbus, Ohio: The Center for Research and Leadership Development in Vocational and Technical Education, The Ohio State University, 1967), pp. 29-47.

Monographs

1. Albert F. Eiss and Mary Blatt Harbeck, *Behavioral Objectives in the Affective Domain* (Washington, D.C.: National Science Teachers Association, 1969), 42 pp.

2. Paul Plowman, *Behavioral Objectives Extension Service* (Chicago, Illinois: Science Research Associates, Inc., 1968-69). See especially:
    Unit 2: "Behavioral Objectives in English and Literature," 28 pp.
    Unit 3: "Behavioral Objectives in Social Science," 37 pp.
    Unit 4: "Behavioral Objectives in Science," 34 pp.
    Unit 5: "Behavioral Objectives in Biology," 29 pp.
    Unit 6: "Behavioral Objectives in Mathematics," 29 pp.
    Unit 7: "Behavioral Objectives in Art and Music," 32 pp.
    Unit 8: "Behavioral Objectives in Reading," 34 pp.

POST-TEST FOR ILP 3

(1) Identify as "behavioral" or "non-behavioral" each of the objectives in the following list (where a "behavioral" objective is defined as one which includes three essential parts—an action, a context, and a criterion of performance):

(a) In a game situation, you should be able to pass a volleyball with a degree of accuracy that permits you to meet a specific placement objective.

(b) For any given Arabic numeral, one through fifteen, the student should know the corresponding Roman numeral.

(c) When you take the next test, you will be given pictures that you should be able to name. You should also be able to draw a ring around the pictures that have the same beginning sound in their names. You should get them all correct.

(d) Pretend you are going to enter a time machine in order to interview Joseph Priestley in his home in Northumberland, Pennsylvania. You should be able to demonstrate your understanding of his scientific, religious, and political contributions and conflicts by writing a list of questions to guide your interview.

(e) Given ten items on a faculty meeting agenda, the teacher should be able to understand what is expected of him.

(2) For each of the above objectives which you labeled as "behavioral," identify each of the three essential parts. For those which you labeled as "non-behavioral," identify or supply each of the parts.

(3) If you are writing an ILP as you read this book, you may already have written statements of major concepts, skills, and values as well as statements of their component parts. In any case, select a component concept, skill, or value and write one or more learning objectives based on the statement you selected.

(4) Describe at least one way each in which learning objectives help to accomplish the following teaching-learning tasks: (a) instructional planning, (b) motivation, and (c) evaluation.

3. Howard J. Sullivan, *Improving Learner Achievement Through Evaluation by Objectives* (Inglewood, California: Southwest Regional Laboratory for Educational Research and Development, undated), 38 pp. (Mimeo.)

Film

Goofing Off with Objectives (by R.F. Mager & H.F. Rahmlow). 14½ min., 16mm, sound, color. Mager Associates, 13245 Rhoda Drive, Los Altos Hills, California 94022, 1969.

E. Do:

Join several of your colleagues in forming a small group for discussion purposes. Consider either or both of the following topics in relation to the objectives for this lesson:

1. In the Teacher's Supplement to this ILP, two basic techniques were described for developing objectives in the affective domain—the "accumulation of behaviors" and "continuum of behaviors" approaches. Which types of general affective objectives lend themselves most readily to each of these techniques? Are both of these methods necessarily tied to long-range evaluation (more than one academic year) of student performance in the area of valuing? Can you devise other ways of developing behaviorally stated affective objectives? Are your answers to any of the above questions influenced by the assumption that affective behaviors are never totally non-cognitive? In what ways does this assumption influence your thinking regarding teaching for affective goals?

2. As you look in the literature on objectives, you will find writers who are both for and against the behavioral approach. Opinion ranges from those who ardently support behavioralizing the curriculum to those who feel that the entire approach is just another fad that will fade away if ignored. Where do you stand? One way to find out is to participate in a forthright discussion with your colleagues after each of you has both written and used learning objectives.

CHECK YOUR PROGRESS

How do learning objectives help both the teacher and the student in instructional planning, motivation, and evaluation?

SELF-TEST KEY

Check your response on the self-test by re-reading answer 4 on the pre-test key for this ILP.

POST-TEST KEY FOR ILP 3

(1)   (a) behavioral   (c) behavioral   (e) non-behavioral
       (b) non-behavioral   (d) behavioral

(2)   The three essential parts of each objective can be identified or supplied as follows. (Of course, in any objective where material must be supplied, you may have written equally valid learning objectives which differ considerably in terms of content from the material given below. However, your ingredients should be of a type which is comparable.)

     (a)   The three essential parts of this psychomotor domain learning objective are as follows:

         Action: *pass* a volleyball
         Context: given a game situation
         Criterion: with a degree of accuracy that meets the specific placement objective

     (b)   The action term used in this objective makes the statement non-behavioral. The statement could be revised as follows:

         Action: *write* the corresponding Roman numeral
         Context: given any Arabic numeral from one through fifteen
         Criterion: all correct

     (c)   The three essential parts of this learning objective are as follows:

         Actions: *name* the pictures and *draw a ring* around those that have the same beginning sounds
         Context: given pictures
         Criterion: all correct

     (d)   The three essential parts of this learning objective are as follows:

         Action: *write* a list of questions
         Context: for personally interviewing Joseph Priestley
         Criterion: the questions should reflect a sufficient understanding of Joseph Priestley's scientific, religious, and political contributions and conflicts so that an effective interview can be secured

(Post-Test Key continued on page 98)

ILP 3—Follow-up

If the results of the self-test for this lesson indicate that you need greater depth, you may wish to review or use more extensively some of the sources suggested under "Learning Activities" in this lesson. If you are satisfied with your performance on the self-test and also with the results of your efforts in actually constructing learning objectives, you may wish to engage in quest. Quest may be undertaken either prior to or following the post-test (page 94) for this ILP.

QUEST

A. Would you like to prepare an affective domain continuum of behaviors similar to the three which were provided in the Teacher's Supplement to this ILP? A great deal of work in affective domain curriculum development is needed. Morris Gall, in the April 1967 issue of the *Grade Teacher Magazine*, identified eight "less tangible goals," as he called them, which need attention. These are as follows:

1. *Self-reliance, self-confidence, and independence* (the self-image). Quality of personality. A child has a sense of psychological security and a disposition to stand by his convictions.

2. *Respect for others.* An appreciation of differences, and a tolerance and acceptance of the ways of others.

3. *Group cooperation.* The ability to work in groups, to share, to lead and follow.

4. *Ability to evaluate one's self.* The development of increasingly refined and accurate standards of personal evaluation.

5. *Critical thinking and judgment.* The process, when confronted with a practical problem, of making a choice, a decision, a judgment or a policy.

6. *Concern for truth.* A disposition to keep an open mind and to raise questions about seemingly established authority.

7. *Self-direction.* Increasing competence in formulating problems and in finding solutions independently.

8. *Ability to communicate.* Development of competence in conveying information, ideas, skills and attitudes to others through the various media of the written and spoken word, the arts, and the sciences.*

*Excerpted from the April, 1967, issue of *Grade Teacher* magazine with permission of the publisher. © 1967 by CCM Professional Magazines, Inc. All rights reserved.

POST-TEST KEY FOR ILP 3 (continued from page 96)

(e) Only the context portion of this objective is adequate according to the standards given in this ILP. The action portion of the objective incorporates a term ("understand") which is not directly observable. This term should be replaced with a more precise one such as that given below. The criterion portion was omitted completely in the original objective. All three portions of the objective could appear as follows:

Action: *describe* the expected behaviors
Context: given ten items on a faculty meeting agenda
Criterion: reach agreement with the other teachers present as to the performance expected of each person

(3) See answer 3 on the pre-test key for this ILP.

(4) See answer 4 on the pre-test key for this ILP.

B. We touched only briefly in this ILP on the important area of motivation. What are the physiological *needs* which precipitate a human being's basic motivational state? How do *needs* evolve into wants and associated motivations? Can a teacher motivate a student or just provide exploratory kinds of experiences which cause the student to change his own motivational state? What implications do your responses to these questions have for providing the kinds of materials, conditions, and relationships which promote learning growth?

If you are satisfied with your achievement on the post-test, you may choose either to return to the quest activities in this ILP or go directly to another ILP. If you decide to go to the ILP which immediately follows this one, you will be taking a logical next step in building your own ILPs. Techniques are presented for organizing media and activities around the concepts and learning objectives which you have already developed.

ILP 4

WHAT WILL FACILITATE THOSE CHANGES?

Individualized Learning Materials and Activities

CONCEPT

The development and use of ILPs are dependent on the selection or construction of individualized learning materials and activities.

SUB-CONCEPTS

Learning materials and activities in ILPs are keyed to specified concepts, sub-concepts, and learning objectives.

Learning materials and activities in ILPs are diversified to allow for individual differences of learners at given curricular levels.

LEARNING OBJECTIVES

Given the concept, sub-concepts, and learning objectives of an ILP, you should be able to select, design, or construct learning materials and activities that correspond to the sub-concept(s) and objective(s) in each ILP lesson.

Given the concept, sub-concepts, and learning objectives of an ILP, you should be able to select, design, or construct diversified learning materials and activities that allow for individual differences of learners at the curricular level for which the ILP is intended.

In ILP 2 we indicated that the pre-test could be placed either in the teacher's materials or in the student's section of an ILP. However, in each of the three ILPs preceding this one, we placed the pre-tests in the teacher's supplement. In this ILP, we altered this pattern to include the pre-test in the student's materials in order to provide a model for this particular variation in format. The number of questions on the pre-test is, of course, irrelevant to the matter of pre-test placement. Rather, placement is a factor of teacher judgment based on the content of the ILP, the level of student responsibility and therefore the amount of teacher-monitoring needed, and the kind of test administration the teacher is able to carry out without detracting from other important instructional duties.

*

It will be noted that in this ILP there are two sub-concepts, two learning objectives, and two lessons. As we indicated in ILP 2, this one-to-one correspondence is the most typical pattern, but it is not essential.

ILP 4—Preliminaries

Take the pre-test which follows. After completing the pre-test, check your answers using the pre-test key which begins on the next page. If you feel, after checking your answers, that you need additional feedback before deciding to do the lessons in this ILP, see your instructor (if available) or obtain an opinion from a colleague and/or a student concerning the learning materials and activities you developed on the pre-test.

PRE-TEST FOR ILP 4

Three different sets of conditions have been established in the three alternative test items provided below. Each set of conditions is consistent with the "given" portions of the two learning objectives for this ILP. Choose whichever set of conditions you wish to employ, and then select, design, or construct diversified learning materials and activities which would help the student achieve the specified learning objective. (In the first and second alternatives, we have supplied the concept and sub-concept statements and the learning objectives. In the third alternative, you are asked to supply these items from the ILP you are constructing as you use this book.)

Pre-Test Alternative #1 (Primary Level)

Concept: Making friends and being thoughtful of others make us happy.

Sub-Concept: Sharing and taking turns help us make friends.

Learning Objective: During class and at recess you will observe and record in writing actions of students in which they shared or took turns and thus helped make someone happy.

Learning Activities: (List the materials and activities that you would use to aid students in attaining the objective.)

1. ....
2. ....
3. ....
4. ....
5. ....
(etc.)

PRE-TEST KEY FOR ILP 4

Any number of appropriate, relevant activities could be listed for each of the pre-test alternatives. The ones which we have presented below are simply a few of many possibilities.

Key to Pre-Test Alternative #1 (Primary Level)

1. DISCUSS ... ways in which you and a friend can have fun with the following things:

    > a box of crayons
    > a swing
    > a book
    > a ball and bat
    > a jumping rope
    > a bag of marbles

2. WRITE ... a story about how you and a friend have had fun together.

3. DRAW AND COLOR ... (with a friend) pictures of things you could share or pictures of children taking turns.

4. PLAY ... at jumping rope and saying the following rhyme:

    > I'll take turns when I play
    > And make it fun for everyone.
    > How many jumps shall I make?
    > One, two, three ...

5. READ OR LISTEN TO ...
    I Learn About Sharing (Nashville, Tennessee: Abingdon Press, 1968), 31 pp.
    Saturday Cat (Minneapolis, Minnesota: T.S. Denison and Company, Inc., 1970), 40 pp.

6. VIEW ...
    Share the Sandpile, filmstrip, black and white. Roa's Films, Milwaukee, Wisconsin.
    Sharing with Neighbors, filmstrip, color. Encyclopaedia Britannica Educational Corporation, Chicago, Illinois.
    Our Class Works Together, 16mm movie, available in either black and white or color. Coronet Films, Chicago, Illinois.

(Pre-Test Key continued on page 106)

Pre-Test Alternative #2 (Secondary Level)

Skill: Changing an automobile tire in a safe and proper manner.

Sub-Skill: Jack up an automobile for tire removal.

Learning Objectives: You will be able to state, orally or in writing, the things you would do to safely jack up an automobile. You will be able to demonstrate correct procedures for properly jacking up an automobile.

Learning Activities: (List the materials and activities that you would use to aid students in attaining the objectives.)

1. ....
2. ....
3. ....
4. ....
5. ....
(etc.)

Pre-Test Alternative #3 (for the ILP you are constructing as you use this book)

Concept or Skill or Value: ....
Sub-Concept(s) or Sub-Skill(s) or Sub-Value(s): ....
Learning Objective(s): ....
Learning Activities: (List the materials and activities that you would use to aid students in attaining the objective[s].)

1. ....
2. ....
3. ....
4. ....
5. ....
(etc.)

PRE-TEST KEY FOR ILP 4 (continued from page 104)

7. RESPOND ... to the following questions based on the goals set in the above books, filmstrips, and movie:

    How do I rate at home?
    How do I rate at school?
    How do I rate with my friends?

8. PLAY ... a game of marbles. Make a circle, use your marbles, and invite someone to play with you.

Key to Pre-Test Alternative #2 (Secondary Level)

1. VIEW ... a film, filmstrip, 8mm film loop, or video tape (either teacher-made or commercially-produced). Filmed material may be selected from those listed in the course bibliography. You are expected to gain information regarding safe steps to follow in changing an automobile tire. (Provision is made for students to check out filmed material to be viewed individually in the film room of the instructional media center.)

2. DO ... a written or oral test on safe procedures for jacking up an automobile. (The student must demonstrate mastery before proceeding to the next learning activity.)

3. DO ... the following in the presence of an experienced adult:

    a. Place a stone, a piece of wood, or some other effective block in front and behind the wheel diagonally opposite the tire to be changed.
    b. Remove the jack, lug wrench, and spare tire from their compartments. Place the tools and spare tire next to the flat tire.
    c. Remove the hub cap with the end of the lug wrench or jack handle. Use the lug wrench to loosen the nuts on the bolts, but do not remove them.
    d. Rest the jack on flat, solid ground or on a flat block of wood. Depending on the design of the jack, raise the axle or the bumper.

*Key to Pre-Test Alternative #3 (for the ILP you are
constructing as you use this book)*

Because you have written your own concept, sub-concept(s), and learning objective(s) for Pre-Test Alternative #3, you (and your instructor) will have to evaluate the learning materials and activities which you developed. The following criteria, plus those in the first learning activity of Lesson 1 in this ILP, are useful as guides:

(1) *relevance* of the learning materials and activities for assisting the student in achieving the learning objective(s),

(2) *diversification* of the learning materials and activities to accommodate individual differences, and

(3) *appropriateness* of the learning materials and activities for potential users.

LESSON 1

SUB-CONCEPT

Learning materials and activities in ILPs are keyed to specified concepts, sub-concepts, and learning objectives.

LEARNING OBJECTIVE

Given the concept, sub-concepts, and learning objectives of an ILP, you should be able to select, design, or construct learning materials and activities that correspond to the sub-concept(s) and objective(s) in each ILP lesson.

The learning activities in this lesson are focused on helping you to conceptualize and gain behavioral competence at "matching" learning materials and activities to sub-concepts and learning objectives. Learning Activity A provides you with critieria which can be used either to critique this match within an existing ILP lesson or to guide the selection, design, or construction of learning materials and activities for a lesson which you are preparing. You are given an opportunity in Learning Activity B to apply these criteria to several sample excerpts from ILPs. In Learning Activity C, you can also obtain practice by applying these criteria to the lessons in this book. Learning Activity D contains two sample learning objectives for which you are asked to specify learning activities. The real test of your behavioral competence occurs in the self-test for this lesson in which you are asked to produce the learning materials and activities for the ILP you are constructing as you use this book.

LEARNING ACTIVITIES

A. Read:

Criteria for Learning Materials and Activities in ILPs

The purpose of learning materials and activities in an ILP lesson is to assist the student in attaining the behavioral competencies described by the learning objective(s). The most difficult part of developing effective learning materials and activities is to make sure that conceptualization actually takes place (rather than rote memorization of verbal concepts). The following series of questions (or criteria) should help you establish conditions so that significant learning can occur.

1. Do the learning materials and activities provide direct perceptual experience with the properties of the objects, processes, and consequences described by the sub-concept statement? If not, do they elicit vivid recall of prior experience with those properties?

2. Do the materials and activities employed operate through sense channels which match the properties about which the student is to learn? (That is, if a student is learning about the scents of perfume, it would be less effective to *talk* about the odor of a particular scent than to use the scent directly via the sense of smell.)

3. Do the materials and activities employed operate through verbal channels when necessary and effective? (That is, verbal channels are necessary for acquiring data and for associating symbols [such as words, musical notation, or numbers] with past perceptions. These verbal channels are used for the purpose of checking or testing perceptions and resultant concept structures by means of verbal exchange with others.)

4. Do student responses required by the materials and activities utilize the following two processes, either separately or in combination: (a) verbal or pictorial responses (i.e., *identifying, naming,* and *describing*), and (b) overt non-verbal executions (i.e., *constructing* an object; *ordering* objects, processes, or consequences in a pattern; and *demonstrating* by performing a task)?

The relationship between the sub-concept statement and the learning objective(s) in an ILP lesson should be clear in the above criteria. The first and second criteria describe the perceptual experience necessary for concept formation. The third and fourth criteria describe the responses which assist concept formation and at the same time provide an on-going student self-check on his attainment of the learning objective(s). These learner responses can be either identical to or analogous to the overt behavior described in the learning objective(s) of the ILP lesson. The behaviors are identical if the response corresponds to the action term(s) in the learning objective(s). The behaviors are analogous if the response is different but supportive of the achievement of the learning objective(s).

To summarize, internal consistency among sub-concepts, objectives, and learning materials and activities in an ILP is highly significant and obviously important. If a given item or activity does not help the student realize in some way the performance specified in the learning objective(s) for an ILP lesson, then it does not belong in that lesson. Of course, no single learning activity should be expected to satisfy all four of the above criteria. But, a group of learning activities for a specific objective should together satisfy the major areas of concern defined in the criteria.

B. Read and analyze:

Sample Excerpts from ILPs

Sample #1—Sub-Concept: Intrusions of magma in the earth's crust are responsible for many igneous formations.

Learning Objectives: Given a drawing of a cutaway section of an igneous region, you should be able to label the section and describe in writing how the igneous formation occurred (the causes).

Given the name of an igneous formation, you should be able to draw a cutaway section of the formation and describe in writing its causes.

Instructions: Do the following learning activities. When you are ready, take the self-test located at the end of the lesson.

Learning Activities:

1. READ . . . "Zone of Fire" from *The Story of Geology* by Jerome Wyckoff (New York: Golden Press, 1960), pp. 30-48.

2. DISCUSS . . . (with a friend working on the same ILP) the cutaway drawing on pages 30-31 of the book listed above. Be able to locate the various igneous formations and explain in writing how they occurred.

3. DO . . . the following worksheet. Check your answers.

Worksheet

1. Lava reaching the earth's surface through long cracks rather than a pipe may simply flow out over the land in wide bubbling rivers called ....

2. Magma forced between rock layers near the earth's surface, thereby causing the top layers to bulge upward, is called a .... when the magma has cooled.

3. Magma that has worked its way between rock layers is called a (a) dike, (b) sill, (c) laccolith, (d) pipe, or (e) neck.

4. Magma that has worked its way upward into a fracture or crack through layers is called a (a) dike, (b) sill, (c) laccolith, (d) pipe, or (e) neck.

5. A channel through which magma rises is called a ....

6. The cup-shaped hole at the top of a cone is called a ....

When a practice exercise, a worksheet, or similar learning activity is planned for student use, such material is often conveniently included in the ILP itself. For example, it might be placed within the learning activities section in which it is initially mentioned (as was done in Sample #1 on page 109). It may also be placed at the end of a given lesson or at the end of the entire ILP. However, it is also possible simply to ask the student to obtain such materials in the instructional media center, at the teacher's desk, or at some other suitable storage location.

Worksheet Key: (1) lava flows, lava lakes, or lava beds; (2) laccolith, batholith, or lapolith; (3) laccolith; (4) dike; (5) pipe; (6) crater.

Sample #2—Sub-Concept: To accomplish the purpose of fictional writing, authors use imagery to appeal to the reader's sense impressions.

Learning Objective: You should be able to identify similes and metaphors in fictional writing.

Instructions: You are required to do Learning Activity 4. You may select from the other learning activities provided below according to your interests and learning needs. When you are ready, take the self-test located at the end of the lesson.

Learning Activities:
1. READ...
   "Imagery" in *Teaching the Novel in Paperback* (New York: The Macmillan Company, 1963), pp. 53-55.
   Seeing and Describing: Selective Descriptive Writing (Lexington, Massachusetts: D.C. Heath & Company, 1966), 128 pp.

2. LISTEN TO...
   Comparisons, audio tape reel. Tapes Unlimited, Detroit, Michigan.
   Metaphor and the Short Story, audio tape reel. McGraw-Hill Book Company, New York.
   Imagery, audio tape reel. Tapes Unlimited, Detroit, Michigan.

3. VIEW...
   Meaning Through Simile and Metaphor, sound filmstrip. Eye Gate House, Inc., Jamaica, New York.

4. READ AND ANALYZE...
   Mark Twain's "Bluejay Yarn" and "The Devil and Daniel Webster." Find examples of metaphors and similes in these works.

Sample #3—Sub-Concept: The heart is a pumping mechanism located in the circulatory system for the purpose of forcing blood through that system.

Learning Objective: Given a diagram of a four-chambered heart, you will be able to identify the separate chambers, the aorta, the vena cava, and the pulmonary artery and indicate the direction of blood flow in each part.

Instructions: You may select any one or more of the following learning activities as you work through this lesson. When you are ready, take the self-test located at the end of the lesson.

Learning Activities:

1. VIEW . . .

    Wonder Engine of the Body, 16mm movie. Bray Studios, Inc., New York.

    Circulation and the Human Body, 16mm movie, available in either black and white or color. Churchill Films, Los Angeles, California.

    The Heart and Circulation, filmstrip, black and white. NASCO, Fort Atkinson, Wisconsin.

2. IDENTIFY AND DESCRIBE . . . (using the diagram included in your ILP or a plastic model from the instructional media center) the separate parts of the heart. Then, in a small group with several other students, discuss the function of each part. Include in your discussion a description of the way the blood comes to and goes from each part of the heart.

3. DISCUSS . . . the appearance of a dissected and labeled heart preserved in a jar. Look at it with a friend and identify each numbered part. Discuss the blood's route through each part of the heart.

4. CONSTRUCT . . . a model of the heart. You will need two large matchboxes (not the covers), two small matchboxes (not the covers), four flexible straws, cellophane tape, red paint, blue paint, and a natural sponge. Use these materials to show the heart both in the way it looks and in the way it works. You may use any reading sources, pictures, specimens, or models that are necessary for you to complete the task.

C. Review and analyze:

Analyzing Learning Activities

Examine the learning materials and activities found in this book. Note their relationship to the learning objective(s) in each lesson. Evaluate the materials and

activities using the criteria found in Learning Activity A in this lesson.

D. Practice:

Writing Learning Activities

Using the objectives provided below, write your own learning activities. Then ask a colleague to read them for their appropriateness and relevancy to the objectives.

Learning Objective #1: Given an outline map of the United States, you will be able to draw, name, and color (according to a basic topography key) the major mountain ranges, lakes, and rivers.

Learning Activities:

1. ....
2. ....
3. ....
4. ....
5. ....
(etc.)

Learning Objective #2: Given a specific destination in the United States, you will be able to demonstrate the use of various transportation schedules in planning a trip from your home to that destination. The travel must occur within a specified period of time.

Learning Activities:

1. ....
2. ....
3. ....
4. ....
5. ....
(etc.)

CHECK YOUR PROGRESS

Using the sub-concepts and related learning objectives that you developed in ILPs 2 and 3, write the appropriate learning materials and activities.

SELF-TEST KEY

Have you provided for perceptual learning as well as for overt verbal and production behaviors? If you have provided only for the latter, you are assuming that your students have already experienced, prior to using your learning materials and activities, the properties of whatever object(s), process(es), or consequence(s) about which you wish them to learn. Evaluate, using the criteria listed in the first learning activity in this lesson, the learning materials and activities you developed on the self-test. If your learning materials and activities do not satisfactorily meet the criteria, justify why they do not.

You are now ready to do Lesson 2 in this ILP. In Lesson 2 you will learn to build the degree of variety and diversity into your learning materials and activities that will accommodate individual differences of learners at given curricular levels.

The content of an ILP is determined when the sub-concepts are specified (see ILP 2, third sub-concept). The learning objectives, materials, and activities simply elaborate the sub-concepts in terms of the learner behaviors expected from conceptualization. For this reason, we will not consider the content question again in this ILP. Rather, at this point we simply assume that content appropriate to an ILP has been identified and that our job now is to focus on that content in order to make it as accessible and relevant to the student as possible. Parenthetically, it should be re-emphasized that alternative choices of content result from allowing students to *choose from among available ILPs, not from diversifying the content within a given ILP*. An ILP should contain diversified learning materials and activities, not diversified content. If it contains diversified content, then it is not an ILP.

LESSON 2

SUB-CONCEPT

Learning materials and activities in ILPs are diversified to allow for individual differences of learners at given curricular levels.

LEARNING OBJECTIVE

Given the concept, sub-concepts, and learning objectives of an ILP, you should be able to select, design, or construct diversified learning materials and activities that allow for individual differences of learners at the curricular level for which the ILP is intended.

Go to the learning materials and activities below. Do as many of the items as are necessary for you to complete the learning objective.

LEARNING ACTIVITIES

A. Read:

Provision for Individual Differences

The most important single facet of an ILP is its built-in provision for individual differences among learners. Provision for individual differences is a necessary response to the observation that people seem to learn in different ways and that they bring differing backgrounds and abilities to the learning task.

Educators frequently use the term "learning styles" as a sort of umbrella term for aspects of individual differences. For example, Frank Riessman described the following three learning styles: (1) visual, (2) oral-aural and (3) physical. You would probably have little difficulty identifying students you have encountered who could be classified primarily in one or another of these categories. However, these classifications are more likely to be descriptive of the particular learning skills which students have or have not developed than of basic differences in learning "styles."

Because students differ in their development of learning skills, it is necessary to provide alternative learning materials and activities in ILPs. For example, field trips, films, and laboratory exercises are primarily "visual" and "physical" in nature and provide students with perceptual experiences. Reading materials are "visual" and "verbal" in character and cause recall of previous experiences. Teacher-pupil conferences and small group discussions are "oral-aural" and "verbal" in character and provide needed feedback to the learner. Activities such as building objects,

creating paintings, composing music, cooking, and participating in simulation games require many types of involvement including "physical," "pictorial," "aural-oral," "non-verbal," and "verbal." ILPs which incorporate a variety of types of learning materials and activities allow the student to choose media to match his existing learning skills or styles, while at the same time they encourage him to learn in new modes.

B. Read and do:

Learning Media: Definitions and Types

The terms "materials" and "activities" have been used in this book to include all possible objects and processes which the learner might employ to achieve his learning objectives. Either term could have been used alone (as has been our pattern in the "Learning Activities" sections throughout this book), or the term "media" could have been used in place of "materials." However, we chose to use both terms in our discussion in this lesson in order to emphasize both objects and processes. In addition, we chose to use the term "materials" because the term "media" is sometimes thought of in the limited sense of only the newer technical aids to teaching and learning.

A basic definition of media is anything which is *intermediary* in getting across an idea. A somewhat fuller definition views media as the devices or methods which are utilized for organizing, presenting, and storing information, and for encouraging appropriate learning responses. Media are systems of communication or aids in the communicative process. However, media, defined in the broadest sense, also include realia from the natural environment (rocks, corn, wood, etc.), artifacts (pottery, paintings, tools, etc.), and, perhaps most important of all, other people. Thus, when we use the term materials, we mean it to include all of the above aspects of the term media.

Although learning materials require learner activity, and vice versa, for the sake of greater clarity we have grouped learning materials and learning activities separately below. Of course, the two lists are necessarily incomplete. *Add to them.* Identify materials (especially realia and artifacts) and activities which are possibly unique to the subjects you teach or to your school or community. Then refer to the lists as you diversify the learning materials and activities in ILPs which you construct. Finally, *work toward the goal of making all of the learning materials in ILPs available to your students on an individual basis as well as on a small or large group basis.*

ILP 4—Lesson 2

Learning Materials

- Art supplies
- Audio tapes
- Books
- CAI programs
- Cards
- Charts
- Chemicals
- Filmstrips
- Games
- Globes
- Kinescopes
- Kits
- Maps
- Microfiche
- Microfilms
- Models
- Movies (8mm, 16mm, and 35mm)
- Musical instruments and scores
- Newspapers
- Periodicals
- Phonodiscs
- Printed matter (text, non-text, pamphlets, etc.)
- Programmed instruction materials
- Slides (35mm, etc.)
- Specimens
- Study Prints
- Transparencies
- Typewriters and other office machines
- Video tapes
- Workbooks

Learning Activities

- Audio recording
- Cooking
- Demonstrations
- Designing and building
- Drama productions
- Field trips
- Filmed productions
- Interviews
- Laboratory experiments
- Painting
- Pupil-teacher conferences
- Role playing
- Sculpturing
- Seminar participation
- Sewing
- Sports activities
- Surveys
- Typing
- Video taped productions

C. Read:

Using Commercial and Non-Commercial Materials

As you develop the learning materials and activities section of an ILP, you will need to include or refer to some or all of the following types of materials: (1) original non-commercial materials of your own, (2) commercially-produced media in the public domain, and (3) commercially-produced media currently under copyright. Items in each of these classes could, of course, be in print or non-print forms.

Non-print materials may be stored in a library, an instructional media center, or in the classroom. Wherever they are housed, it is usually advantageous simply to cite the materials in the ILP (together with instructions for locating and using them) rather than attempting to include them. Of course, there are also times when a complete ILP "kit" is desirable. In general, however, it is better to let the librarian maintain and manage the wide range of non-print learning media needed in ILPs rather than taking the time of the classroom teacher for such duties. In any case, in citing and using such materials, proper credit should be given and copyright regulations should be observed.

Print materials can be included in full in the ILP or they can simply be cited. Original materials which you have written obviously require no citation or footnoting procedures. If print materials in the public domain are included in the ILP, footnoting is necessary. Print materials currently under copyright may be included in full in the ILP only if prior permission is obtained from the publisher and/or authors. However, in all cases, if the print materials are extensive, reproduction in the ILP may be less convenient and/or economical than citing the materials and making them available in the library or, if necessary, in the classroom.

A word of caution is in order concerning original materials. It would indicate inefficient use of the time and talent of teachers involved in the production of ILPs to "re-invent the wheel" by writing their own textbooks. Excellent books, periodical literature, films, filmstrips, programmed materials, and the like are available commercially and should be used whenever appropriate. When it does become necessary to supplement commercial materials with locally produced materials, remember that students are very adept at preparing such materials and that media production activities in ILPs are excellent learning experiences.

D. Select:

Book

>Marshall B. Rosenberg, *Diagnostic Teaching* (Seattle, Washington: Special Child Publications, 1968), 125 pp.

Periodicals

>1. Wayne C. Fredrick and Herbert J. Klausmeier, "Cognitive Styles: A Description," *Educational Leadership,* XXVII (April, 1970), 668-672.

>2. Frank Riessman, "Styles of Learning," *NEA Journal,* LV (March, 1966), 15-17.

>3. "Tools for Teaching," *Forbes,* CII (August 1, 1968), 38-40, 42-44.

>4. Judith Weinthaler and Jay M. Rotberg, "The Systematic Selection of Instructional Materials Based on an Inventory of Learning Abilities and Skills," *Exceptional Children,* XXXVI (April, 1970), 615-619.

Films

>1. *More Different Than Alike,* 16mm, color. National Education Association, Washington, D.C.

>2. *Teaching the One and the Many,* 16mm, color. National Education Association, Washington, D.C.

Multimedia Presentations

>1. *Individualized Instruction: Diagnostic and Instructional Procedures,* color. Oregon State System of Higher Education, Monmouth, Oregon.

>2. *Individualized Instruction: Its Materials and Their Use,* color. Oregon State System of Higher Education, Monmouth, Oregon.

E. Do:

Library Research

Examine one or more major listings of commercially-produced media. Look under topics appropriate to your teaching field and curricular level as an exercise in planning how you might teach a given concept to thirty students who are highly different in terms of motivation, ability, study skill development, interests, emotional development, social needs, physical maturation, and degree of self-directedness. Major media sources that could be used include the following:

1. Educational Media Council, *Educational Media Index* (New York: McGraw-Hill Book Company, 1964), 14 volumes.

2. Carl H. Hendershot, *Programmed Learning: A Bibliography of Programs and Presentation Devices* (Bay City, Michigan: By the author, 1967), issued periodically in supplements.

3. *Learning Directory, 1970-71* (New York: Westinghouse Learning Corporation, 1970), 7 volumes.

4. *Programmed Instruction Guide* (Newburyport, Massachusetts: ENTELEK Incorporated, 1968).

CHECK YOUR PROGRESS

You were asked in the self-test of Lesson 1 in this ILP to write appropriate learning materials and activities for the sub-concepts and related learning objectives that you developed in ILPs 2 and 3. Examine again what you wrote for Lesson 1, but this time concentrate on diversification for individual differences at specific curricular levels. If your learning materials and activities are not sufficiently diversified, you should select, design, or construct additional ones.

SELF-TEST KEY

The following questions will help you evaluate the learning materials and activities you developed for your ILP:

1. Have you provided materials and activities for the student who learns best by visual means? by oral-aural means? by physical means?

2. Have you provided a variety of media at a specific performance level?
3. Is there sufficient range of difficulty in the materials you listed?

As you respond to the above questions, review the lists of possible learning materials and learning activities that were included in this lesson.

POST-TEST FOR ILP 4 and POST-TEST KEY

If you have completed and checked to your satisfaction the self-tests in this ILP, you should be ready for teacher evaluation of your work. Ask your instructor to evaluate your ILP at its current stage of development. If you are using this book without the assistance of an instructor, proceed to Quest or to the next ILP.

However, if you are not satisfied with your results on the self-tests, the fault may be in your having selected a concept and sub-concepts which are particularly difficult to mediate. Try another concept and sub-concepts, write the learning objective(s), and develop learning materials and activities. You may solve whatever problems you are having by simply getting a fresh start, using the new perspectives you have gained thus far.

You are now ready for the post-test for this ILP (opposite page). After completing the post-test, you may wish to pursue a self-initiated quest topic or one of the several that we have provided below. If you choose to proceed directly to ILP 5, you will learn about student evaluation in ILPs. Of course, if our sequence does not fit your immediate needs, you are encouraged to re-examine the contents of the book and follow a different sequence.

QUEST

The following suggestions may be of interest to you in pursuing in depth the topic of learning materials and activities. Of course, these are only suggestions; you may have questions of your own that you would like to investigate.

A. Visit a school, district, regional, or university instructional materials center. Some universities have separate centers for curriculum materials, audiovisuals, and technology.

B. Read in periodical literature, teaching methodology texts, and audiovisual texts about media.

C. Learn more about the effect of computers on education, particularly computer assisted instruction.

D. Explore the multi-sensory approach to planning learning materials and activities.

E. Use the *Education Index* and the ERIC monthly *Research in Education* to find recent information, both theoretical and practical, on topics such as learning strategies, learning models, and learning modes.

ILP 5

WHAT CAN EVALUATION DO TO HELP?

Pre-, Self-, and Post-Assessment

CONCEPT

Pre-, self-, and post-evaluation in an ILP are designed to assess, in a manner consistent with the learning objective(s), the student's grasp of the concept and sub-concepts.

SUB-CONCEPTS

The pre-test is given to the student by the teacher as a prior-to-study method of determining the student's achievement of the learning objective(s). The results of the pre-test are used by the teacher and the student for diagnosis and prescription.

The self-test is taken by the student independently of the teacher as a subsequent-to-study method of determining the student's achievement of the learning objective(s). The results of the self-test are used by the student to assess his need for re-direction of learning effort within a given ILP and his readiness for post-evaluation.

The post-test is given to the student by the teacher as a subsequent-to-study method of determining the student's achievement of the learning objective(s). The results of the post-test are used by the teacher and the student to obtain a measure of growth within a given ILP and to assess the student's readiness for other ILPs.

PRE-TEST FOR ILP 5

(1) Based on the learning objective(s) which you wrote for the ILP you are developing as you use this book, construct pre-, self-, and post-assessment items by which attainment of the objective(s) can be evaluated.

(2) If you were able to do the first pre-test item, your next task is to re-examine the assessment items which you constructed for their consistency with the concept, sub-concepts, and learning objectives in your ILP. Tell how each of these components are related.

(3) Discuss with your instructor (if available) how assessment in an ILP (a) facilitates learning and teaching, (b) encourages intrinsic rewards, (c) provides information for essential records, and (d) provides feedback for curriculum development. If you are using this ILP without assistance from an instructor, discuss with a colleague your ideas concerning each of these outcomes of assessment.

*

This ILP consists of only one lesson. The concept, sub-concepts, and learning objectives are listed in the preliminaries as usual, but the sub-concepts and learning objectives are not repeated at the beginning of the lesson because they all apply to that lesson.

ILP 5—Preliminaries

LEARNING OBJECTIVES

Given the learning objective(s) that you prepared for the ILP you are developing as you read this book, you should be able to construct pre-, self-, and post-assessment items by which student attainment of the objective(s) can be evaluated.

Given the pre-, self-, and post-assessment items which you developed in the first objective for this lesson, you should be able to tell how these items are consistent with the concept, sub-concepts, and learning objective(s) in your ILP.

You should be able to discuss how assessment in an ILP (1) facilitates learning and teaching, (2) encourages intrinsic rewards, (3) provides information for essential records, and (4) provides feedback for curriculum development.

Your next step in this ILP is to complete the pre-test (opposite page). Do not be discouraged if you are unable to complete all of the items on the pre-test. The purpose of the pre-test is simply to help you decide, with assistance from an instructor if possible, which learning activities will be most beneficial to you in learning to write assessment methods and in using the results of testing. If you are using this book independently, make your own decisions based on the information contained in the pre-test key located on the next page.

PRE-TEST KEY FOR ILP 5

There can be no single "key" to the first two pre-test items, as each person's ILP will be different. If you are using these materials without the aid of an instructor, you may wish to ask one of your peers for an additional judgment as to how well the assessment items you wrote relate to the concept, sub-concepts, and learning objective(s) in your ILP. In addition, the first and second learning activities in this ILP are designed to help you with the performances required by the first two learning objectives and the first two pre-test items.

Learning Activity C will help you achieve the third learning objective and the performance required in the third pre-test item in this ILP. In addition, the following list is representative of the kinds of outcomes of assessment that you might have discussed.

Pre-, self-, and post-assessment facilitate learning and teaching in the following ways:
1. Diagnostic information is provided for determining what should be learned in the ILP.
2. Self-assessment helps the student decide whether he needs to re-cycle himself for additional learning activities before taking the post-test.
3. A measure of learning growth is provided by the difference between pre- and post-assessment.

Self-assessment in an ILP encourages intrinsic rewards in the following ways:
1. Self-assessment helps the student set his own specifications for achieving the learning objective(s).
2. Self-assessment forces the teacher to provide students with the time and materials for evaluating themselves.
3. Self-assessment takes the student's focus off the teacher and places it on the learning task.

Assessment in an ILP provides information for essential records in the following ways:
1. Records can be structured to focus on achievement rather than failure.
2. Records can be designed to provide information concerning the student's next steps.
3. Records which incorporate the above two items are excellent for reporting student progress to parents and for maintaining permanent school files.

Assessment in an ILP provides feedback for curriculum development in the following ways:
1. Records can be kept of the percentage of students who have difficulty passing the post-test for each ILP, thereby indicating that one or more learning activities in particular ILPs may need revision.
2. The entire ILP or any of its components can be improved based on student reactions. (See ILP 9 for additional specific types of feedback for curriculum development.)

LESSON 1

Based on your pre-test results, select from the five learning activities provided in the single lesson making up this ILP. When you feel that you have achieved the learning objectives for this ILP, take the self-test.

LEARNING ACTIVITIES

A. Read:

*Writing Test Items Which are Consistent with the
Concept, Sub-Concepts, and Learning
Objective(s) in an ILP*

In practice, a decision concerning the internal consistency between test items and learning objective(s) always begins by re-examining the consistency among the concept, sub-concepts, and learning objective(s). If the learning objective(s) describe student performances which might reasonably be expected to result from a grasp of the concept and sub-concepts, then you are ready to look at the test items themselves.

Test items are written by examining each learning objective and responding to the following three basic questions:
1. What kind of test item(s) require the same behavior as the action term in the learning objective?
2. How can the test item(s) be written so that the required behavior (or action) can occur under the same conditions as those described in the "given" portion of the objective?
3. How can the quantitative and/or qualitative criteria specified in the objective be built into the test item(s)?

Of course, the second and third questions may not refer to explicit parts of a learning objective, but they most certainly would be implied in the objective.

A continuum of six action terms was discussed in ILP 3. When viewed from the perspective of assessment, each of the terms can lead to convergent thinking and production or to divergent processes, depending on the content of the ILP and the nature of the test items. For example, the action term "identify" can result in a convergent behavior in a testing situation such as the following:

Identify on the temperature vs. time graph the boiling point of water.

Conversely, the same action term can result in a divergent behavior such as required by the following test item:

Identify as many uses as you can for a brick.

Thus, inquiry, discovery, and creativity can be encouraged through properly written learning objectives coupled with carefully designed test items. It is equally possible to encourage opposite kinds of behaviors, of course.

If you find, in writing the test item(s) for an ILP, that *only* knowledge-recall type questions are indicated, re-think the learning objectives and the concept and sub-concepts. Revise them if you think it is desirable to do so. But in the end, be sure that the test items call for the same behaviors, conditions, and criteria as the learning objectives.

Learning Activity B contains examples from several subject areas which illustrate each of the points made in this learning activity.

B. Read:

Sample Objectives and Test Items

The learning objectives and test items provided in this learning activity, although taken out of context, are useful as models when you begin to write the test items for your ILP.

1. Creative Writing

    Learning Objective: Given a photograph which contains ten to twelve observable details, you will be able to identify at least eight details and describe them in written paragraph form.

    Assessment Method: Turn to page 56 in *Stop, Look, and Write!* Study the picture carefully. What details do you see? Write one or more paragraphs describing at least eight details which you observe in the picture.

2. English

    Learning Objective: Given sentences, some of which contain hyperbole and some of which do not, you will be able to differentiate accurately between the two.

Assessment Method: Place an "H" in the blank beside each sentence containing hyperbole. Place an "O" in the blank beside each sentence not containing hyperbole.

........John is taller than a TV tower.
........There were countless millions of flowers in the sea.
........Joan was as quiet as a mouse.
........The trees bowed their heads to the storm.
........The happy child ate a mountain of ice cream.
........He speaks in a voice louder than thunder.

3. Physics

Learning Objective: Given numerical values for any two of the following—electromotive force, current, and resistance—you will be able to calculate the third.

Assessment Method: A circuit draws 5 amps at 300 volts. Find the resistance.

4. German

Learning Objective: Given English sentences in the declarative, progressive, and emphatic forms, you will be able to state orally in the present tense the equivalent German sentences.

Assessment Method: State in the present tense the German equivalents of the following:
  I learn German.
  I am learning German.
  I do learn German.

5. Dance and Art

Learning Objective: You will be able to construct a pair of pois for use in the Poi-Poi dance.

Assessment Method: This objective is achieved while the student carries out the learning activities in the lesson. The product, a pair of pois, is evaluated by the teacher for the purpose of post-evaluation. A pre-test would probably be based on student interest. If the student wants to learn to dance the Poi-Poi, he constructs his own pair of pois. If he does not, he selects a different lesson or ILP. Self-assessment could be based on the student comparing his pair of pois with a pair supplied by the teacher.

ILP 5—Lesson 1

6. Industrial Arts

    Learning Objective: Given a piece of stock, you will be able to demonstrate its preparation and mounting in the lathe for faceplate turning.

    Assessment Method: When the student feels he is ready, before, during, or after the appropriate ILP, he contacts the teacher for demonstrating his achievement of the objective.

7. Physics

    Learning Objective: Given a time-distance graph representing uniform straight line motion, you will be able to calculate the speed of an object during the time interval indicated.

    Assessment Method: Calculate the speed of an object during the time interval A,B.

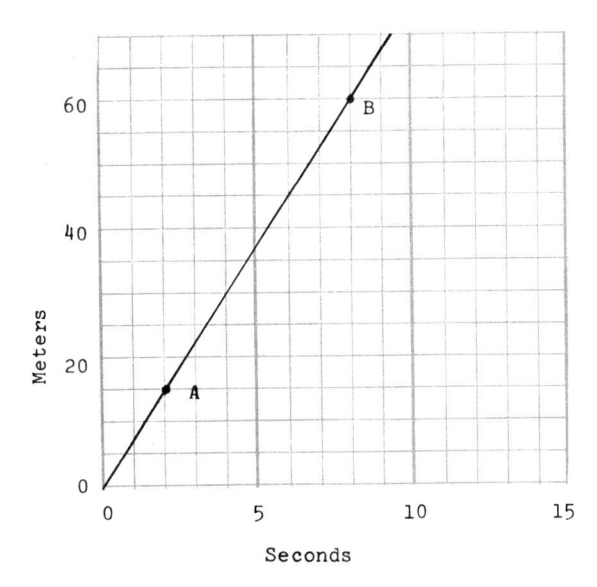

ILP 5—Lesson 1

8. Computer Science

   Learning Objective: Given the standard operational symbols for exponentiation, multiplication, division, addition, and subtraction, you will be able to write all of the corresponding Fortran operation symbols.

   Assessment Method: Write the following number phrases using Fortran operation symbols:

   $3^2 + 6$ .... 1.7×5 ....
   $6 \div 2$ .... $10 - 2$ ....

9. Social Studies

   Learning Objective: You will be able to demonstrate your recognition of the language of prejudice by collecting articles from current print media and by describing in writing examples of radio and/or television programs in which prejudicial language was employed.

   Assessment Method: The product, compiled by the student, is evaluated for its content relative to the language of prejudice.

10. Social Studies

    Learning Objective: You will be able to discuss in a small group session negative and positive effects of automation on the individual. Use specific documented examples which you have identified in your home and community.

    Assessment Method: The student participates in a small group discussion with his peers and teachers.

C. Read:

Outcomes of Assessment in ILPs

When you read the third learning objective for this ILP, you noticed that four outcomes of assessment in ILPs were enumerated. The purpose of this learning activity is to discuss these four outcomes.

Assessment facilitates learning and teaching.—Pre-assessment tells both the student and the teacher whether or not the student has already achieved some or all of the learning objectives in an ILP. Such diagnostic information for *future* learning must be differentiated from diagnostic information for *prerequisite* learning. Because the

student should already have the prerequisites for a given ILP before he takes the pre-assessment for that ILP, the pre-test is designed to determine what the student might already know *in the ILP*. The teacher and the student use this information to diagnose possible learning problems with regard to the learning objectives and to prescribe appropriate learning activities.

Post-assessment occurs subsequent to instruction and self-testing. It is based on the same objectives as pre- and self-assessment and is typically teacher administered. The difference between student behavior on pre- and post-assessment provides the teacher and the student with a measure of the amount and quality of learning which have occurred. If post-assessment reveals that the student has achieved the learning objectives in an ILP, he can move on to his next learning experience. If not, the various remedial alternatives open to the student need to be discussed and a decision made.

We will examine in ILP 8 a "Flow Chart of Continuous Educational Progress Based on Individualized Learning Packages." Some of the alternatives that are available to students and teachers when using ILPs will be pointed out and diagrammed in order to facilitate your understanding of the decision-making process in a continuous progress program. Pre-, self-, and post-assessment provide much of the data which are needed for significant teaching and learning decisions.

Self-assessment encourages intrinsic rewards.—Self-assessment in an ILP should contribute to the student's intrinsic reward system—the reward that he gives himself, for example, as a result of a feeling of accomplishment. There are plenty of opportunities for *extrinsic* rewards in pre- and post-assessment in which the teacher is usually involved. However, when the student evaluates his own learning, apart from the teacher and possibly even his peers, he has little opportunity to derive a reward from others. The reward must come from within. His focus is on the task and his relationship to that task rather than his relationship to the teacher or his peers. If you keep these general principles in mind as you design the self-assessment for an ILP and as you work with students, you will be able to encourage them to develop internal reward systems that contribute to lifelong learning.

Writers such as John Holt (*How Children Fail*) and William Glasser (*Schools Without Failure*) have a good deal to say about our penchant for evaluating students in schools. The following statement by Glasser is very significant, "It's not what other people say of you that's terribly important; it's your impression of yourself, relative to others and to everything else [that is important]." The time that teachers spend evaluating students is much less meaningful than the time students spend evaluating themselves. Glasser adds, "What's very, very necessary is that we spend time evaluating ourselves, and that we set up our schools so that children can spend a great deal of time evaluating *themselves*. In the end, this is what counts."

It is easy to omit self-evaluation in an ILP, but do not give in to the temptation to do so. If something is worth learning, it is worth the student's time to evaluate his achievement of the objective for himself and by himself.

Assessment provides information for essential records.—It is critical, in a continuous progress program, that teachers and students keep track of individual student progress. The kind of format used for a continuous progress record can take many different forms. However, the following types of information are important: (1) the title or concept statement of the ILP being studied, (2) the date started, (3) pre-assessment results, (4) learning activities completed, (5) post-assessment results, and (6) the date completed. Recording of pre- and post-assessment results might be divided into two categories: (1) learning objectives achieved and (2) learning objectives not achieved.

Such records, if properly designed, can also be successfully used as a non-graded report card. The record is updated regularly during small group or individual conferences with each student and, thus, the student has no difficulty explaining such a report card to his parents. Teachers who work together and share responsibility for an individual student's program find such report cards essential in maintaining adequate communication with one another. Of course, continuous progress report cards are just as necessary if ILPs are being used in classrooms operated by only one teacher. If continuous progress learning is to occur, the student's next teacher must know *what* the student has accomplished and not just his estimated success or failure represented by percentages or grade letters.

Assessment provides feedback for curriculum development.—The recordkeeping design suggested in the preceding section provides considerable data that are valuable for evaluating the ILPs themselves. In fact, an ILP can be held accountable for student success through built-in mechanisms for evaluation and modification. If too many students do not achieve a given objective in an ILP, something is wrong with the ILP or with the way the ILP is being used by the student or by the teacher. The alert teacher can also obtain excellent information for modification of the ILP from the kinds of questions students ask and the comments they make while taking the pre-, self-, and post-tests. Some teachers find it useful to keep a notebook in which they record such information for future revision of ILPs. The use of assessment data for curricular improvement will be discussed more thoroughly in ILP 9.

D. Read:

Norm-Referenced vs. Criterion-Referenced Testing

What is the difference in philosophy between the typical testing which occurs in schools and the evaluation which occurs in ILPs? The two sections which follow,

written by Roy A. Moxley (*Educational Technology*, Vol. X, March, 1970, S3-S6), humorously point out the difference.

The Norm-Referenced Test Philosophy
"Well, gang, everyone got over 95 percent correct on that last quiz. Obviously a bad test. It always is when everyone gets everything right or everything wrong. So we're throwing it out and testing you over again.

"I'm going to get rid of all those questions everyone got correct.

"Well, gang, here's the results of a test that's going to count. Fifty percent of the class got over 50 percent correct. It approximated the bell-shape of a normal distribution. Obviously a good test.

"Maybe it's not your fault. It could be genetic. But a lot of you are just lazy. You should—pardon me? Yes, that's right, just leave your drop card on my desk as you leave.

"Those dropouts? I don't want that kind in my class. I want hard-working, intelligent kids. Of course, you're all going to have to work harder on the next test, since we lost a few at one end of our distribution. Only the best are going to survive this course."

The Criterion-Referenced Test Philosophy
"Well, gang, 50 percent of the class got over 50 percent correct. It approximated that bell-shape of a normal distribution. Obviously I had given you a bad program of instruction. We'll try another.

"I'm going to revise all those questions everyone got wrong. Some items may be irrelevant and some may require more discrimination.

"Well, gang, everyone in the class got over 95 percent correct after this new program of instruction. I think congratulations are in order.

"That first test indicated I didn't have a good method of instruction. I should—pardon me? Yes, that's right, just bring your add card next time you come.

"Those old programs? I don't want to use them again. They belong in the wastebasket. Even the present program is going to end up there, as soon as I find a better method. Only the best is going to survive for this course."

E. Select:

Books
1. William Glasser, *Schools Without Failure* (New York: Harper & Row, 1969), 235 pp.
2. John Holt, *How Children Fail* (New York: Dell Publishing Co., Inc., 1964), 181 pp.
3. Norris M. Sanders, *Classroom Questions: What Kinds?* (New York: Harper & Row, 1966), 176 pp.
4. Fred T. Wilhelms (ed.), *Evaluation as Feedback and Guide* (Washington, D.C.: Association for Supervision and Curriculum Development, NEA, 1967), 283 pp.
5. Any good methods books in your own subject field will contain sections on evaluation. Perhaps now is a good time to review those sections if you have not done so recently.

Periodicals
1. Eva L. Baker, "Project for Research on Objective-Based Evaluation," *Educational Technology*, X (August, 1970), 56-59.
2. David Berenson, "How to Find Out What You've Taught Them," *Grade Teacher Magazine*, LXXXIV (April, 1967), 130-132.
3. Caroline M. Dillman and Harold F. Rahmlow, "Writing Sample Test Items for Objectives," *NSPI Journal*, IX (July, 1970), 12-19.
4. William Glasser, "The Effect of School Failure on the Life of a Child, Part 1," *The National Elementary Principal*, XLIX (September, 1969), 8-18.
5. _____, "The Effect of School Failure on the Life of a Child, Part 2," *The National Elementary Principal*, XLIX (November, 1969), 12-18.
6. Roy A. Moxley, "A Source of Disorder in the Schools and a Way to Reduce It: Two Kinds of Tests," *Educational Technology*, X (March, 1970), S3-S6.
7. W. James Popham, "The Instructional Objectives Exchange: New Support for Criterion-Referenced Instruction," *Phi Delta Kappan*, LII (November, 1970), 174-175.
8. Thomas J. Quirk, "Test Scoring Based on the Instructional Objective as the Basic Criterion Unit," *Journal of Secondary Education*, XLV (February, 1970), 61-65.

Filmstrip
W. James Popham and Eva L. Baker, *Evaluation,* 29 min., 43 frames, color. Vimcet Associates, Los Angeles, California, 1967. (This filmstrip is the seventh in a series of seven illustrated filmstrips with accompanying audio-taped narrations that are available from Vimcet Associates.)

CHECK YOUR PROGRESS

(1) As a result of your achievement of the objectives for ILPs 2 and 3, you formulated in writing a concept, sub-concepts, and learning objective(s) for your ILP. You should now construct pre-, self-, and post-assessment items based on the learning objective(s) of your ILP.

Once this task is completed, check to be sure the test items are consistent with the concept, sub-concepts, and learning objective(s). Revise either the test items or the learning objective(s) until the same performance or action and the same conditions are specified in both.

(2) Are you prepared to discuss the outcomes of pre-, self-, and post-assessment? Re-read the third objective for this ILP and think through the points you would want to make in a discussion with another teacher, with students, and with parents.

ILP 5—Lesson 1

SELF-TEST KEY

There is no single "key" to the first self-test item, as each person's assessment items will be different. If you have difficulty evaluating your own achievement, re-read Learning Activity A and apply to your test items the three basic questions listed there.

You can check your response on the second self-test item by using the pre-test key.

If you had difficulty recalling some of the purposes of assessment in an ILP, you probably need to relate more carefully what you have read in this lesson to your own teaching situation. Rather than thinking of groups of students, think about an individual student. What kind of information do you need about his learning progress? What kind of information does the student himself need? What kind of information do his parents need? How, through evaluation techniques, can you maximize his success identity, his development of self-initiative, and his self-direction?

When you feel ready, the post-test for this ILP is located on the next page.

POST-TEST FOR ILP 5 and POST-TEST KEY

Because of the manner in which the learning objectives for this ILP were written, the pre-, self-, and post-tests are identical. Thus, you have already demonstrated your achievement of the learning objectives in the pre- and self-tests. All that remains is for your instructor to check your pre-, self-, and post-test items for the ILP you are constructing, and for you to participate in a small group discussion focused on the outcomes of assessment enumerated in the third objective of this ILP. If you are working independently, read the instructions on the opposite page.

When you are satisfied with your achievement on the post-test, you may choose either to proceed with quest activities in this ILP or, instead, to go directly to another ILP. If you choose to do quest in the area of assessment, several suggestions are provided below. You may wish to go to ILP 6 in which a total view of the nature and function of quest in ILPs is considered. At the conclusion of ILP 6, you should have completed all of the basic parts of the ILP you are developing as you use this book.

QUEST

A. How does our traditional A, B, C, D, and F grading system affect the success vs. failure identity of students? How does it affect a student's concept of himself as a "good person" or a "bad person"?

B. How are people evaluated "on the job" in the world of work as compared to the world of school?

C. What are the values of norm-referenced evaluation as compared to criterion-referenced evaluation?

D. Given the idea that learning objectives specify the conditions under which evaluation will occur as well as the performance expected, how can evaluation be designed to be more relevant to student and adult life outside of school?

E. Are there other specific evaluation topics in which you are interested? If so, state the problems, refine them as necessary, and seek your own resolutions.

ILP 6

WHAT COMES NEXT?
Quest

CONCEPT

The quest section in an ILP is designed to stimulate the student to explore in breadth and/or in depth an area of interest.

SUB-CONCEPTS

In quest activities, decision-making belongs to the student; the learner decides *if* he wants to go into quest, *what* he will be doing in quest, and the *amount and kind* of teacher involvement necessary to the quest activities.

Adequate time for quest must be provided *all* students in order to help them develop the essential qualities of self-initiative and self-direction needed for life-long learning.

LEARNING OBJECTIVES

You should be able to write a definition of quest which includes the basic ideas that are critical to an understanding of the concept.

Given the ILP you are developing as you use this book, you should be able to construct quest opportunities which provide for varying levels of learner independence.

ILP 6—Preliminaries

PRE-TEST FOR ILP 6

(1) Write a definition of quest.

(2) Design, for the ILP you are constructing, at least one quest opportunity at each of three distinct levels of independence in self-initiated and self-directed learning.

Take the pre-test for this ILP (opposite page). Check the test using the key provided on the next page. Based on the pre-test results, you may proceed to the single lesson comprising ILP 6. Or, if the test results indicate that you have already achieved the objectives for this ILP, go on to ILP 7 or to another ILP of your choice.

PRE-TEST KEY FOR ILP 6

(1) Quest is a form of in-breadth and/or in-depth enrichment study that encourages self-initiating and self-directing learning behaviors in all students.

(2) The quest opportunities which you designed for your ILP will differ, of course, depending upon the age level of the intended learner and the subject of the ILP. However, you can use the following three questions to evaluate your quest design:

(a) Does at least one of the quest opportunities provide the student with an already adequately narrowed or delimited problem, leaving the student with only the task of seeking his own learning resources?

(b) Does at least one of the quest opportunities provide the student with a broadly stated problem, leaving the student with the tasks of delimiting the problem and then seeking his own learning resources?

(c) Is at least one of the quest opportunities written in the form of a statement or question that encourages the student to initiate his own problem, delimit it if necessary, and seek his own learning resources?

LESSON 1

If you feel that further study of the concept of quest will help you develop the quest section for your ILP, select from the learning activities provided in the single lesson making up this ILP.

The four learning activities in this lesson begin with an overview of the nature and purpose of quest. The second learning activity contains brief suggestions of what you can do to generate possible quest topics, including interaction with your peers and students, involvement with community patrons, and reading in the professional literature. The third learning activity provides criteria (in addition to those listed in the pre-test key) for evaluating quest topics. The final learning activity suggests sources from which you can select in order to gain greater depth in your understanding of quest.

Proceed to the self-test at the end of the lesson whenever you think you have completed enough learning activities to warrant testing your understanding of the concept of quest.

LEARNING ACTIVITIES

A. Read:

The Nature and Purpose of Quest

The quest section in an ILP includes material that stimulates the student to define a problem for study, to carry out his research, and to achieve an appropriate level of resolution of the problem. These self-initiating and self-directing enrichment activities should operate with a minimum of teacher-imposed structure. Although an ILP as a whole provides a type of structure for the learner, student decisions inherent in using ILPs encourage the development of independence in learning. The quest section in an ILP provides additional opportunities to *expand* the student's skills in initiating and directing his own learning experiences.

Every discipline has its own unique processes of decision making and decision execution. In quest, the student is given an opportunity to learn something about these processes. Quest can vary from the quite simple to the very sophisticated, from library research to laboratory research, from community involvement to literary writing.

Quest is the learner's opportunity to explore an area of interest related to the curricular content of a particular ILP. Quest is *not* a device for taking care of the

brighter students who are able to finish a given ILP before other students working on the same ILP. Enrichment study has too frequently been used as a delaying device in group-paced instructional systems. As a result, many students have developed negative attitudes about independent project work. Unless the student is personally motivated to direct his attention to a quest topic, he soon looks upon such activities as just another form of busy work. Therefore, the student himself must decide whether and how much he wishes to participate in quest.

Some examples might help to clarify the importance of student self-direction in quest. If you have observed a student tinkering with an old gasoline lawn mower engine, you know that such an activity can be a superb form of quest. The activity might be initiated through the quest section of an ILP in which the student is asked how a two- or four-cycle gasoline engine works. Or the student might see the engine in the classroom or at home and ask the question of himself. In any case, once the student begins to investigate—to inquire after—the inner workings of such an engine, it is important that he be left alone. Nothing can destroy a student's interest faster than having a teacher looking over his shoulder asking him questions or giving him directions. In other words, the teacher must avoid re-focusing the student's attention from the learning tasks to the teacher. If the teacher gets involved at all, it should only be to help the student focus his attention on the learning task in a more effective manner.

It should be remembered that quest is a form of personal inquiry. It becomes group inquiry only if the student asks another student to share in the process. When the student is ready for teacher involvement, whether during the investigation or when he feels he has reached some level of resolution that he wishes to check out with his teacher, *he* should ask for the involvement of the teacher.

A second example, which illustrates the fact that age and ability are not criteria for permitting individual self-direction, is that of a child at age one to two who is totally engrossed in removing his shoe laces and attempting to re-insert the laces in the shoe eyelets. Such activities can go on for an hour at a time and may occur repeatedly over a period of many months. However, an adult who offers assistance or distracts the child in any way frequently "turns off" such a quest activity.

A final example illustrates the need for numerous quest opportunities at varying levels of independence if the quality of self-direction is to be developed in students. In science fair projects, the student is expected to initiate a problem, develop hypotheses, design empirical means for testing the hypotheses, summarize and interpret the results, and prepare the project for display. For too many students, science fair projects have been failure experiences because the students had not been given prior practice in independent, self-initiated problem solving. Science teachers, in group-paced instructional settings, generally assign specific pages, problems, and

laboratory exercises and expect their students simply to follow directions. And then, when it is time to prepare science fair projects, they suddenly expect their students to operate independently, an expectation which is unrealistic if the students have not been encouraged to practice such behaviors previously.

How can opportunities for such practice be provided? If you read the left-hand pages of Lesson 2 in ILP 3, you will recall a continuum of five behaviors that relate to valuing independent learning. Three of the behaviors involve concepts, skills, and attitudes that, with minor revision, are descriptive of different levels of quest:

1. Given a delimited quest topic, the student seeks his own resources.
2. Given a broad quest topic, the student delimits the topic and seeks his own resources.
3. Given a self-initiated quest topic, the student delimits the topic as necessary and seeks his own resources.

Typically, both delimited and broad problems should be suggested in the quest section of an ILP, thus providing for the first two behaviors listed above. To provide for the third level of quest, you might write, "Is there a problem that you would like to investigate?" The student would then be free to initiate and carry out a quest problem of his own that would be related to or in some way suggested by the curricular content of a particular ILP.

Before completing this discussion of the nature and purpose of quest, it is important to consider a problem faced by most teachers—that of providing *all* students with *adequate time for quest.* If the teacher's demands on the student's time are too great, the student will feel pressured to spend all of his available time in school just meeting the teacher's objectives for his learning, rather than spending at least part of his time meeting *his own* objectives for his learning. The ILP approach to curricular organization provides built-in expectation for time commitments to quest.

B. Do:

How to Generate Quest Topics

1. Form a small group seminar composed of teachers and students. Discuss the kinds of topics which are appropriate for quest. Try to invent problems which will serve to bridge subject-matter areas. Discuss the feasibility of giving a student credit in all subject areas in which objectives are being met through a given quest activity.
2. Identify resource persons from the community who would be willing to work with teachers in developing quest problems related to the world of work and to social problems within the community. Identify particularly

those adults whose special competencies could be tapped by students whose quest projects have gone beyond the experiences of adults and peers within the school.

3. Search the professional journals to which you subscribe as well as the methods books in your subject field for examples of problems which might be incorporated into the quest sections of ILPs. Keep a card file or notebook in which you list such topics together with problems that your students initiate.

C. Read:

Criteria for Quest

In the pre-test key to this ILP, you were given three criteria to evaluate quest designs. The following six criteria and discussion provide additional guidelines for your development of quest topics. Although the term "independent study" is used in the following quotation, the meaning is essentially the same as that which we have chosen to call "quest."

"1. It [independent study] presents a problem that poses a challenge to the student's curiosity.
2. It encourages the student to discover information he wants to possess, or to explore ideas in which he has an interest.
3. It involves the student in the problem solving process.
4. It inspires the student to ask himself questions whose answers, once obtained, prompt him to ask more questions.
5. It develops in the student a confident attitude toward learning on his own.
6. It gives the student the feeling that he is accomplishing something constructive, worthwhile, and pertinent.

....

"A worthwhile independent study project involves the student in an exploration of a program he wants to explore. It leads him willingly through the problem solving process of collecting, arranging, testing, and evaluating information. It teaches him something he wants to know. It refreshes his inquisitive nature and prompts him to frame new questions about things he still wants to learn.

"Every good independent study project is open at both ends. It possesses an inherent appeal that invites the student to approach it with interest. And when he has finished, it leaves him with the feeling that he would like to do another project equally as attractive."*

---

*"Students Can Learn on Their Own—Let Them," *Croft Professional Growth for Teachers (Science): Junior High School Edition*, Second Quarter Issue, 1966-67, p. 8.

D. Select:

Books

1. William M. Alexander and Vynce A. Hines, *Independent Study in Secondary Schools* (New York: Holt, Rinehart, and Winston, Inc., 1967), 208 pp.

2. B. Frank Brown, *Education by Appointment: New Approaches to Independent Study* (West Nyack, New York: Parker Publishing Co., 1968), 175 pp.

3. Richard S. Crutchfield, "Nuturing the Cognitive Skills of Productive Thinking," *Life Skills in School and Society*, (ed.) Louis J. Rubin (Washington, D.C.: Association for Supervision and Curriculum Development, NEA, 1969), pp. 53-71.

4. Gerald Thomas Gleason (ed.), *The Theory and Nature of Independent Learning: A Symposium* (Scranton, Pennsylvania: International Textbook Company, 1967), 101 pp.

5. Lester C. Mills and Peter M. Dean, *Problem-Solving Methods in Science Teaching* (New York: Bureau of Publications, Teachers College, Columbia University, 1960), 87 pp.

6. Neil Postman and Charles Weingartner, *Teaching as a Subversive Activity* (New York: Delacorte Press, 1969), 219 pp.

Periodicals

1. Richard W. Burns, "The Process Approach to Software Development," *Educational Technology*, IX (May, 1969), 54-57.

2. _____ and Gary D. Brooks, "What Are Educational Processes?" *The Science Teacher*, XXXVII (February, 1970), 27-28.

3. George M. Carnie, "Doing Your Own Thing Via Self-Determined Units," *The Science Teacher*, XXXVII (February, 1970), 35-37.

4. "Students Can Learn on Their Own—Let Them," *Croft Professional Growth For Teachers (Science): Junior High School Edition* (Second Quarter Issue, 1966-67), p. 8.

5. Dorothy Wright, "Try a Quest," *English Journal*, LIX (January, 1970), 131-133, 143.

CHECK YOUR PROGRESS

(1) Can you, in your own words, define quest?

(2) Have you written the quest section for the ILP you are developing as you use this book?

SELF-TEST KEY

(1) One definition of quest was provided on the pre-test key. Another equally useful definition is as follows: Quest consists of suggestions offered the learner that may cause him to initiate self-directed inquiry, in depth and/or in breadth, into additional concepts, skills, and values.

(2) See the pre-test key and Learning Activity C for criteria that can be used to evaluate the quest section in your ILP.

Based on your self-test results, if you feel that you are ready for teacher evaluation, turn to the next page. If you need additional help, discuss your progress and questions with your instructor (if available), or select for additional reading some of the sources suggested in Learning Activity D.

POST-TEST FOR ILP 6

(1) Write a definition of quest.

(2) Design, for the ILP you are constructing, at least one quest opportunity at each of three distinct levels of independence in self-initiated and self-directed learning.

ILP 6—Follow-up

When you have successfully achieved the objectives for this ILP, as determined by the post-test results, give serious consideration to the quest suggestions listed below. Or, if you prefer, proceed to another ILP.

QUEST

The following are suggested quest experiences that you may be interested in pursuing. You are not limited to these topics, however. If you decide to participate in quest, and you are working with an instructor, inform him of your intended activity, including the anticipated starting and completion dates.

A. How can students be provided with adequate time for quest?

B. How can a quest program be effectively administered?

C. How can students be encouraged to participate in quest rather than rushing from one ILP to the next in order to complete as many ILPs as possible?

D. What factors contribute to student responsibility while participating in quest experiences? For example, develop one or more possible formats to assist students in structuring their quest projects or activities.

POST-TEST KEY FOR ILP 6

See the pre-test and self-test keys for possible responses to the first test item and for criteria which can be used to evaluate the quest section in your ILP.

PART III: ORGANIZING THE COMPONENTS
PUTTING THE PIECES TOGETHER!

ILP 7

ORGANIZING FOR ALTERNATIVE INSTRUCTIONAL AND LEARNING APPROACHES

CONCEPT

ILPs may be written for a variety of purposes using three basic formats. "Presentation" and "guided discovery" ILPs are designed to promote specified conceptual learning. "Exploration" ILPs are designed to expand student interests.

SUB-CONCEPTS

In the presentation approach, the concept and sub-concepts are given to the learner in verbal form.

In the guided discovery approach, verbalization of the concept and sub-concepts is withheld from the student but is a focal point for teacher planning.

In the exploration approach, an object or process (rather than a concept or sub-concept) is named as the focus of a single-lesson ILP, and *no* learning objective is specified.

LEARNING OBJECTIVE

Given the three basic formats for ILPs, you should be able to organize (and select or modify as necessary) the ILP components you prepared while using this book so that the "presentation," "guided discovery," and "exploration" approaches to learning are illustrated.

PRE-TEST FOR ILP 7

Using the three ILP formats (but not the accompanying discussion) presented in ILP 7, organize the ILP components you prepared while using this book so that the "presentation," "guided discovery," and "exploration" approaches to learning are employed.

Take the pre-test for this ILP (opposite page). Check the test using the key provided on the next page. If you were only partially successful in using one or more of the three basic formats, you probably will wish to review most of the learning activities in this ILP. Considerable familiarity with, and understanding of, these formats is essential if you are to select and use them efficiently for setting the stage for particular approaches to instruction and learning.

PRE-TEST KEY FOR ILP 7

If you are working with an instructor, ask him to examine your ILP components in each of the three formats. If you are working independently, the following information will help you evaluate the organization of your ILPs.

Presentation Approach.—Because ILPs 1 through 7 in this book are organized according to the presentation format, it is likely that the curricular components you developed as you used this book were oriented toward that approach. If so, you probably experienced little difficulty creating a "presentation" ILP. You may wish to analyze your work in greater detail by comparing its organization and components with ILPs 1 through 7.

Guided Discovery Approach.—As you organized for the guided discovery approach, you may have encountered the need for modifying the learning objectives in your ILP so that "discovery" was not compromised by partial or complete verbalization of the concept or sub-concepts in the objective(s). If you had difficulty changing the learning objective(s) so that the discovery approach could be accommodated, you probably need to review ILP 3 on learning objectives, particularly the action terms in Lesson 2.

Exploration Approach.—Because the exploration approach is designed to promote student encounters with objects or processes, you may find it necessary to develop several single-lesson "exploration" ILPs, depending on the number of such phenomena encompassed by your concept and sub-concepts. Be sure you have named objects or processes that are observable through the senses. In addition, you should compare your "exploration" ILP with ILP 8 in this book, which has been organized using the exploration format.

LESSON 1

The learning activities in the single lesson making up this ILP contain descriptive comments and formats for three basic types of ILPs. The first learning activity concerns the "presentation" format, the second focuses on the "guided discovery" format, and the third describes the "exploration" approach. You should study all three formats and practice organizing ILPs using each one.

LEARNING ACTIVITIES

A. Read:

Presentation Approach

ILPs designed for the presentation approach consist of four basic parts: (1) the Teacher's Supplement, (2) Preliminaries, (3) one or more lessons, and (4) Follow-up materials.

Teacher's Supplement
The Teacher's Supplement contains pre- and post-tests (which normally are controlled by the teacher) and additional information and explanation to assist the teacher. If the pre-test is included in the student's portion of the ILP, it is placed after the "Instructions" section in the Preliminaries. The items of "Additional Information and Explanation" in the Teacher's Supplement are used to (1) suggest methods of identifying those students who would most benefit from an ILP, including interests, prerequisite behaviors, and developmental levels; (2) identify equipment and facilities needed; (3) list complete citations and/or sources of materials; (4) indicate special instructions for evaluation, if needed; and (5) suggest subsequent ILPs.

Preliminaries
The purpose of the Preliminaries is to provide a summary of the concept, sub-concepts, and learning objective(s) for the student. In addition, the "Instructions" section of the Preliminaries directs the student to take the pre-test and tells him how to use the pre-test results for making decisions concerning his subsequent learning tasks.

Lessons
If the ILP consists of only one lesson, the "Sub-concepts" and "Learning Objective(s)" sections are omitted. The purpose of the "Instructions" section is to assist the student in making decisions concerning the learning activities in which he

The next several pages in the Teacher's Supplement contain formats for and descriptive comments concerning two types of projects—"decision making" and descriptive comments concerning two types of projects—"decision-making" and "decision-execution" projects. These formats are included in the Teacher's and "guided discovery" ILPs.

According to Asahel D. Woodruff, decision-making and decision-executing, together with exploration of one's surroundings, constitute most if not all of the daily behaviors of people in the real world. Therefore, projects focused on developing these two types of behaviors are important keys to greater relevance in the curriculum. Such projects contribute to increased student motivation and, as a result, to the increased effectiveness of existing ILPs. In addition, ILPs written specifically to support decision-making and decision-execution projects speed the transition to a more meaningful curriculum of the type described in the following two sources:

1. Philip G. Kapfer, Miriam B. Kapfer, Asahel D. Woodruff, and Rowan C. Stutz, "Realism and Relevance—Payoffs of the Life-Internship Approach," *Educational Technology*, X (November, 1970), 29-31.

2. Philip G. Kapfer, Miriam B. Kapfer, Asahel D. Woodruff, and Rowan C. Stutz, *Toward the Life-Internship Curriculum* (Carson City: Nevada State Department of Education, 1971), 60 pp.

Decision-Making (or Process) Projects

The format for a decision-making project must not be confused with an ILP. Rather, this format represents a procedure for making a rational decision within which ILPs are used to provide the conceptual learning necessary to support that process. Hopefully, the decision is one the student wants to make, thus solving the motivational problem. The decision-making format has two uses—one in quest and the other as a teacher-structured guide for providing practice in decision-making for students.

Quest

If the student elects to engage in a quest activity that involves making a decision, he may use the decision-making format independently of the teacher. Thus, he would (1) state the problem, (2) identify alternative solutions or proposals, (3) investigate the alternative proposals by structuring his own learning activities or by using ILPs which are available, (4) identify the probable consequences of each solution, and (5) make his decision. He would be evaluated for the quality of his decision-making process, *not* for making the right decision.

(Continued on page 196)

will engage. Required learning activities (if any) are specified. If all the learning activities are optional, this is also stated. You will notice that directions for each learning activity are contained within the activities themselves and *not* in the "Instructions" section which precedes all of the learning activities.

Follow-up

The "Instructions" section in the Follow-up format directs the student to the post-test and contains information that will help him make a decision concerning his subsequent activities based on the post-test results. The "Quest" section may be placed among the Follow-up materials (as illustrated in the following format) or it may be placed in the Lessons section after the self-test key.

(Continued from page 194)

Teacher-Structured Guide

The decision-making project is designed to help resolve the process vs. product controversy currently (and recurrently) being waged in the professional literature. It is virtually impossible to separate process and product, as any product (such as conceptual learning) is necessary for a creative process to occur and is modified constantly by that process. Similarly, creative process is modified by the demands of a particular product (such as the conditions surrounding a decision which must be made).

The teacher may pre-structure a decision-making project to any degree he wishes, depending on the maturity and experience of his students. For example, the teacher may (1) state the problem, (2) identify alternative solutions, and (3) construct and list the ILPs (using either the presentation or guided discovery approaches) that will help the student (1) identify and state the probable consequences of each solution and (2) make his decision. Or, the teacher may provide less structure by omitting from the student guide sheet the content of any of the sections that he wants the student to develop for himself.

(Continued on page 198)

ILP 7—Lesson 1

FORMAT FOR THE "PRESENTATION APPROACH"

(1) Teacher's Supplement

    PRE-TEST

    ....
    ....
    ....

    PRE-TEST KEY

    ....
    ....
    ....

    POST-TEST

    ....
    ....
    ....

    POST-TEST KEY

    ....
    ....
    ....

    ADDITIONAL INFORMATION AND EXPLANATION

    ....
    ....
    ....

(Continued from page 196)

FORMAT FOR THE STUDENT GUIDE SHEET IN A "DECISION-MAKING PROJECT"

PROBLEM STATEMENT
....
....
....

ALTERNATIVE SOLUTIONS OR PROPOSALS
    1. ....
    2. ....
    3. ....
    etc. ....

LEARNING ACTIVITIES OR ILPs THAT WILL PROMOTE DECISION-MAKING
    1. ....
    2. ....
    3. ....
    etc. ....

PROBABLE CONSEQUENCES OF EACH SOLUTION
    1. ....
    2. ....
    3. ....
    etc. ....

DECISION (Which solution or proposal seems to offer the most of what you want? Be prepared to justify your decision with sound information.)
....
....
....

(Continued on page 200)

ILP 7—Lesson 1

(2) **Preliminaries**

CONCEPT

....
....
....

SUB-CONCEPTS

1. ....
2. ....
3. ....
etc. ....

LEARNING OBJECTIVE(S)

1. ....
2. ....
3. ....
etc. ....

INSTRUCTIONS

....
....
....

(Continued from page 198)

Decision-Execution (or Production) Projects

The format for a decision-execution project, as was true of the decision-making project, must not be confused with an ILP. Rather, the format represents a procedure for producing something the learner wants, and ILPs provide the conceptual or motor skill learnings which support that production. A decision-execution project may be used whenever the student wants to produce a physical object, an aesthetic object, a developed idea, a description, a condition, a planned event, an argument, a proposal for action, or the like. The decision-execution format also has two uses—one in quest and the other as a teacher-structured guide.

Quest

If the student elects to engage in a quest activity that results in any of the products named above, he may use the decision-execution format. He would (1) name the product, (2) state its specifications (it is at this point that creativity is involved), (3) specify the steps necessary in production, and (4) structure his own learning activities or use ILPs which are available. He would be evaluated for his accomplishment of the project according to specifications.

Teacher-Structured Guide

As with the decision-making project, the decision-execution project is designed to help resolve the process vs. product controversy. Rephrasing an earlier statement, products (such as physical objects) evolve as a result of creative processes and are modified constantly by those processes. Similarly, creative processes are modified by the demands of particular products.

The teacher may, of course, pre-structure a decision-execution project to any degree he wishes by filling in all of the sections in the format or by leaving some of the sections blank. As in the decision-making project, the most important task that the teacher performs is in promoting meaningful projects and in identifying and constructing ILPs which will help the student successfully to *make* and *execute* decisions.

(Continued on page 202)

(3)   Lessons

   ILP.....   LESSON.....

   SUB-CONCEPT(S)
   ....
   ....
   ....

   LEARNING OBJECTIVE(S)
   ....
   ....
   ....

   INSTRUCTIONS
   ....
   ....
   ....

   LEARNING ACTIVITIES
   1.   ....
   2.   ....
   3.   ....
   etc. ....

   SELF-TEST
   ....
   ....
   ....

   SELF-TEST KEY
   ....
   ....
   ....

(Continued from page 200)

FORMAT FOR THE STUDENT GUIDE SHEET IN A "DECISION-EXECUTION PROJECT"

OBJECTIVE (The name of the product.)
....
....
....

SPECIFICATIONS FOR THE PRODUCT
    1. ....
    2. ....
    3. ....
    etc. ....

STEPS NECESSARY TO PRODUCE THE PRODUCT
    1. ....
    2. ....
    3. ....
    etc. ....

LEARNING ACTIVITIES OR ILPs THAT WILL PROMOTE DECISION EXECUTION (PRODUCT DEVELOPMENT)
    1. ....
    2. ....
    3. ....
    etc. ....

(4) **Follow-up**

INSTRUCTIONS
....
....
....

QUEST
1. ....
2. ....
3. ....
etc. ....

B. Read:

Guided Discovery Approach

As was the case in the presentation approach, the guided discovery approach consists of four basic parts: (1) the Teacher's Supplement, (2) Preliminaries, (3) one or more lessons, and (4) Follow-up materials.

Teacher's Supplement
In some cases, psychologists believe that a concept cannot be transmitted in verbal form from a teacher to a student. Rather, the student must construct his own concepts from the inputs received through his perceptual experiences. However, the teacher must know where to focus the attention of the student, and for this reason a clear conceptual statement is needed for teacher use. Hence, the concept and sub-concepts are placed in the Teacher's Supplement in the guided discovery approach. The remaining parts of the Teacher's Supplement are the same as in the presentation approach.

Preliminaries
The "Learning Objective(s)" section in the Preliminaries provides a summary of the behavior changes the student is seeking to make. The "Instructions" section contains the same type of information as in the presentation approach. As was the case in the presentation approach, the pre-test may be placed after the "Instructions" in the Preliminaries rather than in the Teacher's Supplement.

Lessons
If the ILP consists of only one lesson, the "Learning Objective(s)" section is omitted. The purpose of the "Instructions" section is the same as in the lesson format for the presentation approach.

Follow-up
The Follow-up materials for the guided discovery approach are the same as in the presentation approach.

FORMAT FOR THE "GUIDED DISCOVERY APPROACH"

(1) Teacher's Supplement

CONCEPT

....
....
....

SUB-CONCEPTS
1. ....
2. ....
3. ....
etc. ....

PRE-TEST

....
....
....

PRE-TEST KEY

....
....

POST-TEST

....
....
....

POST-TEST KEY

....
....
....

ADDITIONAL INFORMATION AND EXPLANATION

....
....
....

(2) Preliminaries

LEARNING OBJECTIVE(S)

1. ....
2. ....
3. ....

INSTRUCTIONS

....
....
....

(3) Lessons

ILP..... LESSON.....

LEARNING OBJECTIVE(S)

....
....
....

INSTRUCTIONS

....
....
....

LEARNING ACTIVITIES
1. ....
2. ....
3. ....
etc. ....

SELF-TEST

....
....
....

SELF-TEST KEY

....
....
....

(4) Follow-up

INSTRUCTIONS
....
....
....

QUEST
1. ....
2. ....
3. ....
etc. ....

C. Read:

Exploration Approach

The exploration format is a greatly simplified single-lesson ILP. Its purpose is to stimulate interest rather than to promote achievement of a specific learning objective.

Even though the exploration format is not structured around a concept and sub-concepts, it is conceptual in nature. It differs from the presentation and guided discovery approaches in that the teacher is not attempting to direct the nature of concept formation that will occur. Rather, the student is allowed to perceive the structural and functional properties of an object or process. Conceptualization is a natural product of such encounters, and necessarily differs from one learner to the next.

The exploration format is useful at all levels and is relatively easy to construct and use. The teacher simply names an object or process with which he wants his students to become familiar. He describes it in a manner that will communicate to his students in terms of their immediate environment. Then, he provides instructions to guide student selection of learning materials and activities that involve direct perceptual experience with the properties of the object or process. Finally, the student summarizes, either orally or in writing, what he learned about the object or process. During this stage, the teacher's task is to attempt to identify deeper interests which may have resulted from the exploration process and to suggest other possible ILPs or projects in which the student might wish to become involved.

FORMAT FOR SINGLE-LESSON ILPs USING THE "EXPLORATION APPROACH"

ILP.....

OBJECT OR PROCESS ....

BRIEF DESCRIPTION
....
....
....

INSTRUCTIONS
....
....
....

LEARNING ACTIVITIES
1. ....
2. ....
3. ....
etc. ....

STUDENT SUMMARY OF WHAT WAS LEARNED
....
....
....

ILP 7—Lesson 1

CHECK YOUR PROGRESS

Practice synthesizing ILPs using three basic approaches and formats—"presentation," "guided discovery," and "exploration." In the three types of ILPs you construct, utilize in the original or modified form the ILP components you developed as you used this book.

SELF-TEST KEY

See the pre-test key for guidance in evaluating your work. For greater detail, see the discussion sections preceding each of the three ILP formats.

If you are satisfied with your self-test results, take the post-test (next page).

POST-TEST FOR ILP 7 AND POST-TEST KEY

If you are working with an instructor, ask him for evaluation and feedback concerning the three ILPs you organized as you used ILP 7. If you are working independently, evaluate your own work based on the content of ILP 7.

When you have completed the post-test and are satisfied with the results, you may wish to select a quest topic from those listed below or initiate a topic of your own. Otherwise, you may proceed to another ILP.

QUEST

A. Do you have some ideas for constructing your own formats for organizing the curricular components of ILPs?

B. What kinds of variations might be incorporated into the three ILP formats provided in this ILP?

C. What kinds of transition formats could you develop for assisting a faculty in moving from conventional practices to an individualized curricular approach?

D. Read the left-hand pages (in this ILP) concerning decision-making and decision-execution projects. What is the relationship of ILPs to such projects? How does a life-oriented combination of ILPs and projects provide for the development of creative skills and process skills in the learner?

ILP 8

NEW TEACHER-LEARNER ROLES IN AN INDIVIDUALIZED LEARNING PACKAGE SYSTEM

(Exploration Approach)

PROCESS

Steps and decisions while using ILPs.

BRIEF DESCRIPTION

ILPs are used by the teacher to establish the conditions under which the student can focus his attention on a task and set about to achieve that task in a self-paced, individualized manner. In order to accomplish this, directions must be clear so that the student knows what steps to follow and what decisions to make, either independently or with assistance from his teacher.

INSTRUCTIONS

Three learning activities are provided below. The first involves direct observation and perception and the second is verbally oriented. The third provides optional readings.

After completing the learning activities, summarize what you learned in the space provided on page 229 under the heading "Student Summary of What Was Learned." Then ask your instructor to evaluate your summary and help you decide what your next learning task should be. If you are working independently, choose your next learning experiences based on the stage of your ILP production activity and your implementation needs.

LEARNING ACTIVITIES

1. *Observe a continuous progress program in operation.* Locate a continuous progress program in your locale. Make arrangements to spend one or two days observing and analyzing student and teacher roles. Also, compare the student materials being used with the ILPs described in this book. You will find it helpful to use some type of checklist or guide to assist you while making your classroom observations. Such instruments are designed to help the observer focus on the salient characteristics of classroom conditions. In addition, they promote the collecting of data which can be verbalized in an objective and specific manner subsequent to the observation period. One such instrument, the "Analytical Record of Teaching," may be found in *A Teaching Behavior Code* by Asahel D. Woodruff and Janyce L. Taylor. Copies are available from the Utah State Board of Education, Salt Lake City.

2. *Read the paper entitled "Flow Chart of Continuous Educational Progress Based on ILPs."* For your convenience, the paper has been included in this book beginning on page 231. This learning activity will help you *conceptualize* and verbalize the *perceptual* experiences you had while doing the observation and analysis specified in Learning Activity 1.

3. *Select from the following sources.* The materials cited below contain additional information about individualized programs. Although they are not all focused exclusively on teacher-learner roles, you should analyze them for the affects that varying approaches to individualized instruction have on such roles.

   Books

   a. C.M. Lindvall and John O. Bolvin, "Programed Instruction in the Schools: An Application of Programming Principles in Individually Prescribed Instruction," *Programmed Instruction*, Sixty-sixth Yearbook of the National Society for the Study of Education, Part II (Chicago, Illinois: University of Chicago Press, 1967), pp. 217-254.

   b. National Education Association Center for the Study of Instruction, *Rational Planning in Curriculum and Instruction: Eight Essays* (Washington, D.C.: National Education Association, 1967), 203 pp.

   c. Louis J. Rubin (ed.), *Life Skills in School and Society*, 1969 Yearbook of the Association for Supervision and Curriculum Development (Washington, D.C.: The Association, 1969), 171 pp.

d. Melvin M. Tumin, "Ability, Motivation and Evaluation: Urgent Dimensions in the Preparation of Educators," *Preparing Educators to Meet Emerging Needs,* (eds.) Edgar L. Morphet and David L. Jesser (Denver, Colorado: The Dingerson Press, Inc., 1969), pp. 1-18.

Periodicals

a. Thorwald Esbensen, "Student Learning Contracts: The Duluth Model," *Educational Screen and Audiovisual Guide*, XLVIII (January, 1969), 16-17, 35.

b. John C. Flanagan, "Functional Education for the Seventies," *Phi Delta Kappan*, XLIX (September, 1967), 27-32.

c. Richard V. Jones, Jr., "Learning Activity Packages: An Approach to Individualized Instruction," *Journal of Secondary Education*, XLIII (April, 1968), 178-183.

d. Philip G. Kapfer, "An Instructional Management Strategy for Individualized Learning," *Phi Delta Kappan*, XLIX (January, 1968), 260-263, 43.

e. Jan McNeil and James E. Smith, "The Multi's at Nova," *Educational Screen and Audiovisual Guide*, XLVII (January, 1968), 16-19, 43.

f. Thomas J. Ogston, "Individualized Instruction: Changing the Role of the Teacher," *Audiovisual Instruction*, XIII (March, 1968), 243-248.

g. Arthur B. Wolfe and James E. Smith, "At Nova, Education Comes in Small Packages," *Nation's Schools*, LXXXI (June, 1968), 48-49, 90.

Film

Rx for Learning. 30 min., 16mm, sound, color. Learning Research and Development Center, University of Pittsburgh. (Distributed by William W. Matthews & Co., Century Building, 130-134 Seventh Street, Pittsburgh, Pennsylvania.)

STUDENT SUMMARY OF WHAT WAS LEARNED

FLOW CHART OF CONTINUOUS EDUCATIONAL PROGRESS BASED ON ILPs

(Printed consecutively on right- and left-hand pages)

The "Flow Chart of Continuous Educational Progress Based on ILPs" is designed to help teachers and administrators conceptualize (1) the flexibility of ILPs for continuous educational progress, and (2) the more personalized and, therefore, more humanized teacher and student roles which result from using ILPs. In other words, the Flow Chart is a workable plan for using ILPs in courses or programs structured to achieve continuous student progress.

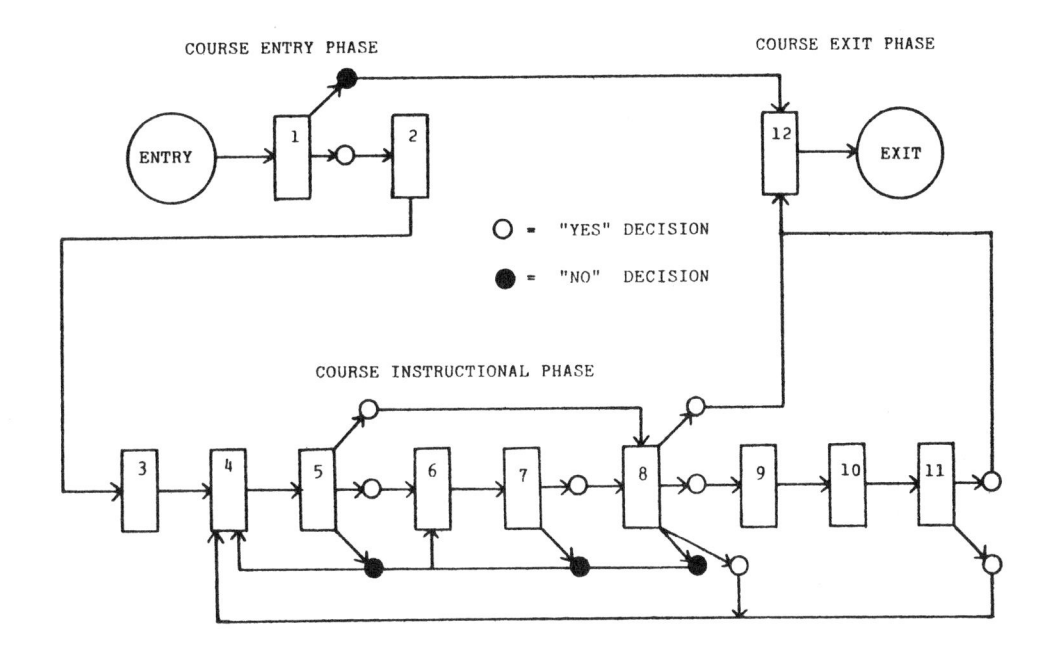

(1) Course Pre-Assessment
(2) Course Orientation
(3) Introduction to ILPs
(4) ILP Selection
(5) Pre-Assessment in an ILP
(6) Learning Activities
(7) Self-Assessment in an ILP
(8) Post-Assessment in an ILP
(9) Quest Topic Selection
(10) Quest
(11) Quest Topic Resolution
(12) Course Post-Assessment

Figure 2—Flow Chart of continuous educational progress based on ILPs.

Continuous Educational Progress Flow Chart

How may the Flow Chart be interpreted? Even the most flexible flow chart can be interpreted as inflexibly, of course, as the user may wish. To the methodologically rigid person, "pupil-teacher decisions" become teacher decisions, and "pupil options" become teacher-determined requirements (or "singular prescriptions"). The Flow Chart can also be interpreted for practically any system of instruction, including group-paced procedures. However, the explanatory material which follows the Flow Chart clarifies the fact that its most important applications lie in the area of individualized programs.

A preliminary inspection of the Flow Chart reveals three distinct sections—the Course Entry Phase (upper left), the Course Instructional Phase (lower center), and the Course Exit Phase (upper right). In the interests of simplicity, only "yes" and "no" decisions are shown in the Flow Chart. In this regard it should be remembered, however, that "yes" and "no" are simply convenient terms for flow chart use. As far as the student and the teacher are concerned, many variations on these decisions actually exist, including deviating from the ILP entirely. (This type of deviation from relatively sequenced learning materials and experiences has been referred to as an individual "system break"—a necessary and healthy expression of the changing profile of an individual's capacity.) Some of the alternative decisions might include the following: "I am ready to go on to the next part of this ILP," "I can skip some parts of this ILP because I already have achieved these objectives," "I do (or do not) wish to do quest study in this area," "I misjudged in selecting this ILP and want to get out of it and into one that is not quite so advanced," and so forth.

The following sections are devoted to detailed descriptions of teacher and student roles at each of twelve intermediate steps in the Flow Chart, plus the entry and exit steps. Frequent reference to the Flow Chart itself is essential as each step is considered.

Entry Step
"Entry" indicates entering a course or area of study. Students may enter at any point in time, not just at the beginning of a semester or school year. Grade levels no longer exist. Artificial boundaries separating the academic disciplines also disappear.

Step 1: Course Pre-Assessment
A pre-assessment instrument covering the content of an entire course is administered based on the learning objectives established for the student to achieve in the course. The results of the pre-test are recorded.

If the pupil is not ready for the course, the professional staff makes a "no" decision. Or, if the pupil already has achieved the course objectives and should receive "credit by examination," the professional staff makes a "no" decision. In the event of either of these two "no" decisions, which would be confirmed at Step 12 by a course post-test, the professional staff routes the pupil to another course or area of study. If the professional staff determines that the pupil is ready to proceed to Step 2, a "yes" decision is made. The "yes" or "no" decision is recorded together with the reason for the decision.

Pre-assessment for a course contributes to individualization of instruction by assuring success experiences for each student. Such evaluation is sufficiently predictive (1) so that failure experiences resulting from study in areas for which the student is not prepared are avoided, and (2) so that boredom and wasted time resulting from study in areas in which the student has already achieved the learning objectives are minimized.

Step 2: Course Orientation
During this step, students are oriented to instructional procedures for the course. The concept of continuous progress based on ILPs is introduced and explained. Course orientation is designed to familiarize students with their new roles—with the learning behaviors expected of them—in individualized instructional settings. The orientation system is organized so that students at varying levels of self-initiative and self-direction in independent learning are dealt with at their own levels and are assisted, on a long-range basis, in becoming more autonomous in their learning behaviors. In addition, basic nuts-and-bolts operating procedures necessary to administer an individualized program are communicated to students. Storage and retrieval of ILPs, classroom procedures for forming temporary learning teams, sign-up systems for pupil-teacher conferences and small group discussions, and flexible scheduling programs are examples of the standard operating procedures with which students are familiarized. The importance of pupil-teacher conferences, especially with reference to decision-making points in the Flow Chart, is emphasized during course orientation.

Step 3: Introduction to ILPs
Students are introduced throughout the course to ILPs which are available. Techniques such as field trips, information on current events, guest speakers, and mediated sources are used for presenting materials to stimulate pupil interest in conceptual and skill areas covered by (or extending from) the course. In the process of motivating and introducing students to available ILPs, the teacher is alert to his new role. He does not lecture to "cover the course"—rather, he organizes to uncover it.

Step 4: ILP Selection
Based on Step 3 (the introduction to students of available ILPs) and teacher-student consultation concerning course pre-test results, the student selects an ILP in which he is interested. The ILP selected and the date of selection are recorded. As a part of

the process of ILP selection, students maintain, with the help of their teachers, nongraded record systems in which information is kept concerning *what students can do* when evaluated rather than *what they cannot do*. Such systems serve the dual functions of providing a device for monitoring student progress and reporting to parents.

Until the student has met all course requirements, *he returns to Step 4 each time he is ready to select a new ILP.*

Step 5: Pre-Assessment in an ILP
After an ILP has been selected, a pre-assessment instrument for the ILP is administered and the results are recorded. The ILP pre-test results are discussed by the teacher and the student. An important aspect of the teacher's role is to conduct small group discussions and individual conferences in order to assist students in the decision-making processes associated with using ILPs. During the student-teacher conference, a decision is made as to whether the student will proceed to Step 8 and take the post-test for the ILP ("yes" decision). Or, the student may proceed to Step 6 and participate in learning activities ("yes" decision). Or, he may return to Step 4 and select a different ILP ("no" decision). The "yes" or "no" decision is recorded together with the reason for the decision.

If the student proceeds to Step 6, a tentative post-test date is established for the "terminal" learning objectives in the ILP as well as "en route" monitoring dates for the learning objectives which must be evaluated along the way. An integral part of such "contracting" relates to tailoring the teacher-set performance level specified in each objective to the needs of the individual student.

Step 6: Learning Activities
When the decision is made for the student to continue in an ILP, he proceeds to Step 6, the learning activities. He completes any required learning activities and selects from among the others according to his interests, learning "style," and ability. Students working in the same ILP may form discussion groups or learning teams of approximately two to five persons. Student-teacher conferences are held to assist the student in focusing on the learning task, to obtain the student's reaction to the learning materials and activities, and to assist in monitoring and recording the student's progress.

Step 7: Self-Assessment in an ILP
When the student believes that he has achieved the learning objectives in Step 6, he uses a self-administered and self-scored assessment instrument. Based on the results of the self-test, the student determines if he should proceed to Step 8 and take the ILP post-test ("yes" decision), or re-cycle to Step 6 for further learning activities in the same ILP ("no" decision), or re-cycle to Step 4 and select a different ILP ("no"

decision). The "yes" or "no" decision is recorded together with the reason for the decision.

An important phase of the teacher's role is to maximize for the student the possibility of success. This is the reason for tailoring to each student's ability and needs the performance-level expectations of the learning objectives.

The student's role in the self-assessment process is to evaluate himself so that he might better know himself and guide his own behavior. Much goal-directed behavior is learned behavior. The student should have many experiences related to measuring his progress toward goals that others have set for him as well as toward goals that he has established for himself.

Step 8: Post-Assessment in an ILP
If the student decides in Step 7 that he is ready for the post-test, he informs the teacher of this fact. The post-test is then administered and the results are recorded. A student-teacher conference is held to compare pre- and post-test results and to make necessary decisions concerning future tasks. After successfully completing the post-test, the student may proceed to Step 9 and engage in quest activities ("yes" decision), or he may re-cycle to Step 4 and select a different ILP ("yes" decision). If the student has completed all of the course objectives, he may proceed to Step 12 and exit from the course ("yes" decision).

If the test results were *not* satisfactory, one of two "no" decisions is necessary. The pupil may re-cycle to Step 6 to study further in the same ILP or he may re-cycle to Step 4 and select a different ILP. The "yes" or "no" decision is recorded together with the reason for the decision.

Any system needs its own self-correcting mechanisms. Through self-assessment, the student already knows whether or not he has achieved the ILP learning objectives. The teacher, however, also needs feedback. With such data, his role becomes that of an action researcher who is seeking information for improving the content and use of ILPs.

Step 9: Quest Topic Selection
If the student elects to participate in quest, he selects a project (problem or product) for enrichment study that is related in some way to the previous ILP studied. The project selected is recorded, and any subsequent changes in the nature of the project are recorded. Students contemplating similar projects may form learning teams of approximately two to five persons.

Step 10: Quest
In quest, the student becomes immersed, at his own level of sophistication, in the

processes of inquiry and/or production characteristic of a particular area. The teacher's role in quest is to avoid excessive amounts of direction that are apt to increase the dependence levels of students. Where quest ends and teacher-directed learning begins, however, is of much less concern than is the wholehearted involvement of a student in the search for an answer to a question which has become *his* problem or in the development of a product that *he* wants. If desired, small group discussions are held for the purpose of sharing quest experiences. The student records his own progress during quest, and the teacher monitors that progress. Pupil-teacher conferences are held whenever necessary.

Step 11: Quest Topic Resolution
A pupil-teacher conference or small group discussion is held to examine the student's resolution of the problem that he studied or to evaluate the product that he produced. The results of the conference or discussion are recorded.

Then, a decision is made as to whether or not the pupil has met all the course objectives. If so, the pupil proceeds to Step 12 and to the exit phase ("yes" decision). If all of the course objectives have not been met, the pupil is re-cycled to Step 4 and assisted in selecting another ILP ("yes" decision). The nature of the "yes" decision is recorded together with prescribed next steps for the student to take.

Step 12: Course Post-Assessment
A post-assessment instrument covering the content of an entire course is administered based on the learning objectives established for the student to achieve in the course. The course post-test is constructed so that a measure of course effectiveness is obtained together with the measure of student achievement. The results of the post-test are recorded.

The post-test for a course does not differ in nature from the post-test for an ILP. Both are based on behaviorally stated learning objectives. Both are sampling devices, but at different levels. Both should be sufficiently diagnostic to permit identification of areas in which further work is or is not needed. And both are taken by the student when he and the teacher feel that the student has achieved specified objectives and is ready for post-assessment.

Exit Step
"Exit" indicates leaving a course because the student has achieved the objectives of the course at levels appropriate to him. When the student has completed one area of study, he is ready to move on to another. The time of the school year in which this occurs is completely unimportant. In other words, credit is not obtained by a process of "homesteading." "Squatter's rights" to promotion from one grade to the next or for a unit of credit is not an appropriate concept in a continuous progress, individualized curricular structure.

PART IV: EVALUATION FOR DECISION AND ACTION
IMPROVEMENT NEVER ENDS!

ILP 9

EVALUATING THE INDIVIDUALIZED CURRICULUM AND THE CONTINUOUS PROGRESS SYSTEM

CONCEPT

The evaluation of ILPs, and of the continuous progress system under which they are used, creates opportunities for improvement.

SUB-CONCEPTS

The internal consistency and organization of ILPs can be improved through the application of standard evaluation criteria.

The use of ILPs in continuous progress systems can be improved through the application of standard evaluation criteria.

LEARNING OBJECTIVES

Given criteria for evaluating the internal consistency and organization of ILPs, you should be able to demonstrate (1) that your ILPs contain all the necessary curricular components, and (2) that those components are consistent with each other.

Given criteria for operating individualized programs, you should be able to evaluate your current program and construct changes where necessary.

PRE-TEST FOR ILP 9

(1)   Examine the ILPs which you constructed as you used this book. Do they meet the following criteria?

.....(a)   Are all elements present in each of your ILPs (according to the three formats presented in ILP 7)?
.....(b)   If any elements are not present, should they be?
.....(c)   Are the elements in agreement with accepted knowledge in the curricular area in which you work?
.....(d)   Is the curricular content of each element consistent with or relevant to each other element?
.....(e)   Does each element communicate? For example, will students be able to understand what they see and read, and will they know what they are expected to do?
.....(f)   Have individual differences among students been considered? In other words, are the elements applicable to an appropriate range of student abilities, learning "styles" or skills, perceptual-conceptual backgrounds, and motivational states?

(2)   An extensive list of major and component criteria and performance objectives for evaluating individualized instructional programs is provided in the second learning activity in this ILP. Using this list, record "yes" or "no" beside each of the following numbered blanks to indicate whether or not your present instructional program meets the stated criteria for individualization.

Intellectual and Physical Development

1-a. ....
1-b. ....
2.   ....
3.   ....
4.   ....

(Pre-Test continued on page 242)

ILP 9—Preliminaries

Take the pre-test for ILP 9 (opposite page). If you are using this book with the assistance of an instructor, he may wish to conduct the pre-test during either a small group discussion or an individual conference.

When you have completed and checked the pre-test, proceed to the single lesson comprising this ILP. If you feel that you have already achieved the objectives for ILP 9 and, therefore, that you do not need the learning experiences incorporated in this ILP, go on to the quest section or to another ILP (if you studied the ILPs in this book in other than numerical order).

PRE-TEST FOR ILP 9 (continued from page 240)

Social, Emotional, and Value Development

1-a. ....
1-b. ....
2.   ....
3-a. ....
3-b. ....
4.   ....

Teaching-Learning Systems

1. ....
2. ....
3. ....
4. ....
5. ....
6. ....
7. ....

Evaluation Systems and Change Processes

1. ....
2. ....
3. ....
4. ....

LESSON 1

You should do the first two learning activities in this lesson. Subsequently, you may select from the remaining two learning activities as needed to build your understanding and background.

LEARNING ACTIVITIES

A. Do:

Evaluation of ILPs

A summary list of criteria for evaluating ILPs was included as the first item in the pre-test for this ILP. A considerably expanded list, primarily synthesized from the preceding ILPs, is presented below. Use the list to evaluate the consistency and organization of the ILPs you have developed. In the evaluation process, you may wish to prepare a separate sheet of paper with numbers corresponding to the criteria listed below.

As you examine your ILPs, enter a score of 0 to 4 next to the corresponding criterion number in order to quantify your qualitative judgment. Use the scores as follows: 4 = excellent, 3 = good, 2 = fair, 1 = poor (but adequate for student use and feedback), 0 = not present (or, if present, not acceptable for student trial).

The following code will be placed after each criterion to indicate the ILP approach(es) to which the criterion applies: P = "presentation," GD = "guided discovery," and E = "exploration."

Major and Component Ideas (Concept and Sub-Concepts)

1. Are the concept and sub-concepts stated simply and completely? (P, GD)
2. Are the concept and sub-concepts written at the language level of the proposed learner? (P)
3. Are the sub-concepts logical and relevant segments of the concept? (P, GD)
4. Are the sub-concepts manageable within a single ILP? (P, GD)
5. If motor skills are involved, is each discrete operation enumerated? (P)
6. Are objects and processes named simply and clearly? (E)

PRE-TEST KEY FOR ILP 9

Because responses to both of the pre-test questions will vary for each person, a specific pre-test key is not provided. If you are working with an instructor, he will evaluate your responses to the pre-test items (after visiting your classes, if possible). If you are using these materials without the aid of an instructor, you may wish to ask one of your peers for an additional judgment concerning the ILPs you have constructed or concerning the instructional program in your classroom or school.

Learning Objectives
1. Are the learning objectives stated simply and completely? (P, GD)
2. Are the learning objectives written at the language level of the proposed learner? (P, GD)
3. Are actions described that can reasonably be expected to result only if the desired conceptualizations have occurred? (P, GD)
4. Are the intended outcomes described specifically enough so that evaluation is possible, but not so specifically as to result in segmented, non-functional behaviors? (P, GD)
5. Do the learning objectives require verbalization only, or do they describe desired processes or products that would result from familiarity with the structural or functional properties of things (such as the common properties of objects, the interaction of objects, or the consequences of interacting objects)? (P, GD)
6. Are the conditions specified under which evaluation will occur? (P, GD)
7. Are the qualitative and/or quantitative expectations clearly stated or implied? (P, GD)

Learning Materials and Activities
1. Will the learning materials and activities help the student realize the performances specified in the learning objectives? (P, GD)
2. Do the learning materials and activities provide direct perceptual experiences with the properties of objects, processes, and/or consequences? If not, do they elicit vivid recall of prior experiences with those properties? (P, GD, E)
3. Do the materials and activities employed operate through sense channels that match the properties about which the student is learning? (P, GD, E)
4. Do the materials and activities employed operate through verbal channels when necessary and effective? (P, GD, E)
5. Do student responses required by the materials and activities utilize the following two processes, either separately or in combination: (a) verbal or pictorial responses, and (b) overt non-verbal executions? (P, GD, E)
6. Have materials and activities been provided for the student who learns best by visual means? by oral-aural means? by physical means? (P, GD, E)
7. Has a variety of materials and activities been provided at each of several specific performance levels? (P, GD, E)
8. Is there sufficient range of difficulty in the materials and activities listed? (P, GD, E)

Evaluation

1. Do the test items call for behaviors identical to the action terms in the learning objectives? (P, GD)
2. Are the conditions (the "givens") during testing the same as those specified in the learning objectives? (P, GD)
3. Does pre-testing provide diagnostic information for determining what should be learned in an ILP (in other words, which objectives have already been met and which have not)? (P, GD)
4. Does self-testing help the student decide whether he needs to re-cycle himself for additional learning activities before taking the post-test? (P, GD)
5. Does the difference in response between pre- and post-testing provide a measure of learning growth? (P, GD)
6. Does self-testing help the student set his own specifications for achieving the learning objectives? (P, GD)
7. Does self-testing take the student's focus off the teacher and place it on the learning task? (P, GD)
8. Do testing procedures focus on achievement rather than on failure? (P, GD, E)
9. Do test results help the student determine his next steps in learning? (P, GD, E)
10. Is the transition from testing to reporting student progress smooth and logical? (P, GD, E)
11. Does testing provide feedback for continued curriculum development? (P, GD, E)

Quest

1. Does quest provide for decision-making and/or decision-executing projects? (P, GD)
2. Does at least one of the quest opportunities provide the student with an already adequately narrowed or delimited project, leaving the student with only the task of seeking his own learning resources? (P, GD)
3. Does at least one of the quest opportunities provide the student with a broadly stated project, leaving the student with the tasks of delimiting the project and then seeking his own learning resources? (P, GD)
4. Is at least one of the quest opportunities written in the form of a statement or question that encourages the student to initiate his own project, delimit it if necessary, and seek his own learning resources? (P, GD)
5. Are the quest options designed at appropriate levels of complexity? (P, GD)
6. Will the quest options hold student interest long enough to encourage attainment? (P, GD)

Organization

1. Are your ILPs organized according to the formats in ILP 7? Can the modification or omission of any of the elements be justified? (P, GD, E)
2. Will students be able to understand what they see and read? In other words, will they know what they are expected to do in an individualized program that incorporates your ILPs? (P, GD, E)
3. Are the ILPs attractively designed? (P, GD, E)

B. Do:

Program Evaluation

This learning activity is designed to assist you in evaluating your current instructional program and in planning for its improvement. Four major criteria together with component criteria and performance objectives are provided on the following pages. The criteria and objectives may be used to evaluate a single classroom or a total school program. They may also be used by individual teachers and administrators as well as by teams of educators.

As you proceed through the evaluation instrument, record ideas for specific ways in which a school might demonstrate achievement of each of the listed performance objectives. (It will soon become apparent that the objectives are written at a sufficiently abstract level to permit demonstration of achievement in a variety of ways, thus preserving both a program's uniqueness and the possibility for creativity within it.) After you have completed this task, rank the performance objectives that you feel your particular school could not presently meet, according to the order in which you would like to work toward their achievement.

*Instrument for Evaluating Individualized Programs**

Major Criteria	Component Criteria	Performance Objectives
A. *Intellectual and physical development.* — The school program provides for the intellectual and physical development of students.	1. Students are provided opportunities to develop proficiency in those content areas that are specified by district and state curricular requirements.**	1-a. You should be able to *demonstrate* that district and/or state curriculum guides are being implemented.** 1-b. You should be able to *demonstrate* that district and/or state instructional requirements specified in documents other than curriculum guides are being met.**
	2. The student's instructional program is commensurate with his conceptual capacity.	2. You should be able to *demonstrate* that instructional programs are being implemented that provide for variations among students in their capacities for conceptualization.
	3. The student's instructional program is commensurate with his motor skill development.	3. You should be able to *demonstrate* that instructional programs are being implemented that provide for variations among students in their motor skill development.

*Adapted from materials prepared by P. Kapfer, M. Kapfer, *et al.*, for the Clark County School District, Las Vegas, Nevada, 1969.

**It is assumed that curriculum guides or other official sources specifically designed to support individualized curricular programs are available.

ILP 9—Lesson 1

Major Criteria	*Component Criteria*	*Performance Objectives*
(continued)	4. Feedback from students and the community influences curricular offerings.	4. You should be able to *demonstrate* that students and the community are able to influence curriculum development.
B. *Social, emotional, and value development.*—The school program provides experiences that focus on the social needs, emotional needs, and value development of all students.	1. The instructional program provides for the social development of students.	1-a. You should be able to *demonstrate* that instructional programs include social learning activities (e.g., small group discussions, team projects, teacher-pupil conferences, school government, and civic action projects). 1-b. You should be able to *demonstrate* that minority group students are provided opportunities to participate in instructional programs with all other students.
	2. The instructional program provides for the emotional needs and well-being of students.	2. You should be able to *identify* programs specifically designed to provide students with opportunities to be involved with and be responsible for the well-being of other students.

ILP 9—Lesson 1

Major Criteria	*Component Criteria*	*Performance Objectives*
(continued)	3. The instructional program provides for the development of positive and realistic self-images on the part of students.	3-a. You should be able to *demonstrate* that the instructional program is becoming increasingly responsive to the needs of students for successful learning experiences at their own levels of ability.
		3-b. You should be able to *demonstrate* that reward rather than punishment is the primary means used to influence student operant behavior.
	4. The student's instructional program is commensurate with his affective growth and ability.	4. You should be able to *demonstrate* that students have program alternatives from which they can choose, based on their interests, attitudes, and values.
C. *Teaching-learning systems.*—The school program utilizes teaching-learning systems which focus on students as active, individual, unique learners.	1. Individually unique curricular sequences are provided each student.	1. You should be able to *identify* instructional materials and/or methods being implemented that permit each student to advance (as he demonstrates readiness and according to his own unique route) (a) from one learning experience to the next within a course and (b) from one course to the next.

ILP 9—Lesson 1

Major Criteria	Component Criteria	Performance Objectives
(continued)	2. Student assignments are experience oriented.	2. You should be able to *demonstrate* that students are provided opportunities to interact with the objects, processes, and consequences from which concepts and skills are derived.
	3. Curriculum design provides for problem solving, discovery, and inquiry methods.	3. You should be able to *identify* instructional materials and/or methods being implemented that provide students with opportunities for problem solving, discovery, and inquiry approaches to learning.
	4. Opportunities for independent work are provided that are appropriate to the varying needs and abilities of students.	4. You should be able to *demonstrate* that individual student tasks contribute to reinforcing and/or increasing the ability of students to handle independence in learning.
	5. A multimedia approach to instruction is used.	5. You should be able to *demonstrate* that media of all types are available to individual students as well as to groups of students.

ILP 9—Lesson 1

Major Criteria	*Component Criteria*	*Performance Objectives*
(continued)	6. A variety of instructional techniques are used.	6. You should be able to *demonstrate* that student assignments include a variety of methods such as large group lectures, small group discussions, independent study, laboratory activities, simulation, individual conferences, field trips, and so forth.
	7. Students are informed of the teacher's objectives.	7. You should be able to *demonstrate* that learning objectives are communicated to students.
D. *Evaluation systems and change processes.*—The school provides a positive environment for continuous evaluation and change.	1. Assessment methods provide information that facilitates student tasks designed to meet the needs and/or desires of individual learners.	1. You should be able to *demonstrate* ways in which you are using assessment methods to identify the needs and/or desires of students.
	2. Students are provided opportunities to evaluate their own progress.	2. You should be able to *demonstrate* ways in which you are providing students with opportunities for self-evaluation.
	3. Assessment methods result in reporting systems to parents that focus on objective measures of behavior change.	3. You should be able to *demonstrate* that parents are informed of their child's specific behavioral growth.

Major Criteria	Component Criteria	Performance Objectives
(continued)	4. Assessment methods assist teachers in evaluating techniques and materials used by teachers and students.	4. You should be able to *demonstrate* that you select and revise objectives and learning activities based both on an analysis of available resources and on results from student assessment.

*

C. Do:

Self-Analysis Instrument

In ILP 1 a learning activity was provided that was designed to facilitate assessment of the curricular vehicles that you currently are using in your classroom or school. As a result of the experience you gained while using this book, your responses to the items in the self-analysis instrument should have changed. Return to Learning Activity B in ILP 1 (Lesson 1) and re-evaluate your current (or projected) program.

D. Select:

Books

1. *Evaluative Criteria for Small Group Instruction, School Within a School, Large Group Instruction, Modular Schedule, and Independent Study* (Abington, Pennsylvania: Abington High School, North Campus, undated), 53 pp.

2. Ira J. Gordon (ed.), *Criteria for Theories of Instruction* (Washington, D.C.: Association for Supervision and Curriculum Development, NEA, 1968), 44 pp.

3. Hulda Grobman, *AERA Monograph Series on Curriculum Evaluation: Evaluation Activities of Curriculum Projects* (Chicago, Illinois: Rand-McNally & Company, 1968), 136 pp.

4. Norman V. Overly (ed.), *The Unstudied Curriculum: Its Impact on Children* (Washington, D.C.: Association for Supervision and Curriculum Development, NEA, 1970), 130 pp.

5. Ralph W. Tyler, Robert M. Gagné, and Michael Scriven, *AERA Monograph Series on Curriculum Evaluation: Perspectives of Curriculum Evaluation* (Chicago, Illinois: Rand-McNally & Company, 1967), 102 pp.

Periodicals
1. Clark C. Abt, "How to Compare Curriculum Materials: An Evaluation Model," *Nation's Schools*, LXXXVI (July, 1970), 21-28.

2. Samuel Messick, "Educational Evaluation as Research for Program Improvement," *Childhood Education*, XLVI (May, 1970), 413-414.

3. William E. Turner, "A Plan to Appraise Individual Progress for Continuous Learning," *The Elementary School Journal*, LXIX (May, 1969), 426-430.

4. Ralph W. Tyler, "New Dimensions in Curriculum Development," *Phi Delta Kappan*, XLVIII (September, 1966), 25-28.

CHECK YOUR PROGRESS

If you have completed to your satisfaction Learning Activities A and B, you are ready for the post-test.

Take the post-test (following page). When you have successfully achieved the objectives for this ILP, as determined by the post-test results, you may wish to select one of the quest suggestions provided below or you may identify a quest topic of your own.

QUEST

A. How would you organize an entire faculty to conduct a school self-assessment based on the instrument provided in Learning Activity B in this ILP? How would you use the results of such an assessment?

B. What support services for teachers are needed at the district and building levels to implement an individualized instructional program?

C. Have you been stimulated, as a result of your study of ILP 9, to investigate any topics not mentioned above that are related to the individualization of instruction?

POST-TEST FOR ILP 9 AND POST-TEST KEY

If you are working with an instructor, ask for feedback concerning your responses to the evaluative criteria supplied in Learning Activities A and B. If you are working independently, ask a teacher or administrator colleague for assistance.